A CENTURY OF EXCELLENCE

100 GREATEST PACKERS OF ALL TIME

Vicki?
From
one Packer
fan to
another
Mike Jacquart
Pola, WB consh

By **Mike Jacquart**

Design by **Shawn Williams**

Write it Right LLC
Iola, WI 54945
www.writeitrightllc.com

Ordering Information:
Quantity sales. Special discounts are available on quantity purchases by corporations, associations, and others. For details, contact the publisher at the address above.
Orders by U.S. trade bookstores and wholesalers. Please contact Write it Right LLC:
Tel: 715-445-4386; mjacquart@writeitrightllc.com or visit www.writeitrightllc.com

Printed in the United States of America

Publisher's Cataloging-in-Publication data
Jacquart, Mike.
A Century of Excellence : 100 Greatest Packers Of All Time

p. cm.
ISBN 9781-7978-79-765
1. The main category of the book — History — Other category. 2. Another subject category — From one perspective. 3. More categories — And their modifiers. I. Johnson, Ben. II. Title.
HF0000.A0 A00 2010
299.000 00–dc22 2010999999

First Edition

14 13 12 11 10 / 10 9 8 7 6 5 4 3 2 1

PREFACE

Bart Starr. Brett Favre. Ray Nitschke. Reggie White. Aaron Rodgers. Surely any Packers fan would place them among any list of Packers greats. But who would they add to round out a top 20? And, since we're in the midst of the Packers' 100th anniversary celebration, why stop at 20? How about a top 100? And how would someone go about ranking these players? Since I love the Packers, and sports lists, the seed was planted for writing A Century of Excellence: 100 Greatest Packers Of All Time.

I am a big fan of Packers' history (which was instilled in me by my father) ...and here's the kicker: I must admit it was doubly enjoyable to pour through profiles of Packers greats in a losing season that many fans would just as soon forget.

A Packers loss on Sunday in 2018? Rather than simply being frustrated about losing yet another close game, I was able to take a trip down Memory Lane to better times... years when Lombardi-led teams won FIVE championships. Years when Mike Holmgren-coached squads earned SIX straight playoff appearances and a third Super Bowl title. To a Mike McCarthy-led FOURTH Super Bowl win. Wanting this book to be as complete as possible, I also learned more about the Curly Lambeau championship years. (After all, the coach and founder of the Packers steered the team to SIX championships in the pre-Super Bowl era.)

Younger Packers fans are spoiled. All they've known are successful teams, so the current back-to-back losing seasons (2017-2018) have to be pretty shocking. You have to go way back to the Lindy Infante era (1990-91) to witness Packers teams with back-to-back sub .500 teams!

Of course, we older fans knew plenty of heartaches in decades past. Consider: From the time Lombardi left in 1968 to when Mike Holmgren arrived in 1992, the Packers had FIVE winning seasons. FIVE! (1969, 1972, 1978, 1982, 1989) and only '72 and '82 marked playoff appearances. In those days, 8-8 was a pretty darn good season!

But losing, not winning, has been the rarity in the past 25 years. And yet, even back in the day when Packers teams were seldom anything to get excited about, they always had some talented players that were fun to watch. John Brockington. James Lofton. Paul Coffman. Lynn Dickey. Sterling Sharpe. To name but a few.

There have been a LOT of great players who've worn the Green and Gold over the years. Celebrating those players and their accomplishments is the point of A Century of Excellence: 100 Greatest Packers Of All Time. While the focus is on the "top 100", the standout play of some additional Packers is also recognized in chapters later in this book. All in all, it's a reminder what a truly unique franchise the Packers — and its players — really is.

MIKE JACQUART

INTRODUCTION

At first, it didn't seem that coming up with 100 greatest Packers would be all that difficult. Could I even come up with 100 players? But a quick online search on a football database revealed nearly fifty current and former Packers in the letter "A" alone!! Clearly, determining the 100 greatest Packers ever would involve more research than I had envisioned!

As a result, I had to come up with some criteria. Such measures are always rather subjective to be sure, but it was still necessary to have some sort of determining factors:

* I wanted the list to be as representative of different eras as possible – not just those from the Lombardi years to the present.

* I ruled out former Packers who mainly played for other teams, and/or who only played for the Packers for a single season. Thus, you won't find players like NFL Hall of Famers like Emlen Tunnell or Ted Hendricks on this list. (They do, however, show up in a different chapter.)

* Similarly, if the ex-Packer had only one really great season in the Green and Gold, he didn't make the cut either. My reasoning was that, with only 100 players out of more than 1,000 who have suited up in a Packers uniform, I would have to leave out many players who had multiple productive years with the Pack, so how could I include a "one-season wonder", at least on the main "top 100" list?

* I determined that it was necessary to take the opinions of others' into account – therefore, Packers who have been inducted into the team's Hall of Fame were strongly considered. (Packers HOFers are indicated with an asterisk.) However, in some instances the important role of a certain player took precedence, regardless of whether he has a HOF bust.

* Conversely, active players were not given high priority. The reason? A current player has not had an entire career, so his ranking could go up – or down in the future. (There was one notable exception. Bet you can guess who?)

* I wanted to have this list as representative of different positions as possible. That was not entirely possible because there have been more great players at some positions than others. Still, the goal was to include linemen and other unheralded players, not just their more well-known brethren like quarterbacks, running backs, and WRs.

* It's worth noting that this list was a work in progress in many aspects until the version you are seeing now. There are players on previous lists who did not make the "final cut." Running backs James Starks and Eddie Lacy are among them. Why? Leaving them in would have meant bumping out DB Al Harris and G Josh Sitton, and since both of them were All-Pros in their careers, that did not make a lot of sense to me. Other players on original lists but eventually excluded were "old-timers" Fred Cone, Jug Earp, and Tiny Ingebretsen.

* Still other Packers "made the cut" but their ranking moved up, or down – for various reasons, mostly due to how they fit into the list overall. Clay Matthews, for instance, while terrific early in his Packer career, has been pretty average in recent years, which knocked down his stock slightly. On the other hand, other players I would not initially have rated as highly – such as Bobby Dillon and Gale Gillingham, were bumped up when research turned up more laurels for the players than I had realized.

* In addition, there were a number of players I had a difficult time leaving off of this list, but in the end I did. Among them were A.J. Hawk and Bubba Franks. Hawk, in particular was a tough scratch because he is the Packers' all-time leading tackler. However, unlike John Anderson, whose tackling record Hawk broke, Anderson also intercepted 25 passes in his Packers' career, while Hawk seldom made a big play in a game. He was steady, yes, which weighed in his favor – but he still had a rather nondescript career for that high of a draft choice. Speaking of steady, that also defined Franks – especially in the red zone, where he was a large target for Packer QBs. But it was not possible to include every good former Packer on this list! (Hence, ten Honorable Mention picks appear in this book – as well as some additional players – they just weren't among the top 100, that's all.)

* Do you agree with these omissions? After reading this entire list, let me know who you think were some particularly good – or bad – selections by emailing **mjacquart@writeitrightllc.com**.

I hope you enjoy this trip down Memory Lane.

MIKE JACQUART

TABLE OF CONTENTS

100-90

GREATEST PACKERS OF ALL TIME

Creative Commons, creativecommons.org/licenses/by-sa/2.0/deed.en

100 AL HARRIS, CB
(PACKER YEARS 2003-2009)

Adept at press coverage, who will ever forget his electrifying game-winning interception return in the Packers' 2003 playoff win over the Seahawks? Harris was acquired in a trade with the Philadelphia Eagles following the 2002 season. A two-time Pro Bowl selection, Harris's long, stringy deadlocks proved to be a fashion statement for other NFL players.

Card and Coin/Packer City Antiques

99 WAYNE SIMMONS, LB
(PACKER YEARS 1993-97)

An overlooked defensive standout, the first-round draft pick out of Clemson brought a nastiness to some celebrated Packers' defensive units, which featured shutting down opposing teams' tight ends. Wayne Simmons set the tone for the Packers' defense early in the 1995 divisional round win over defending champion San Francisco, when he forced a 49er fumble on the game's first play, which cornerback Craig Newsome picked up and ran in for a touchdown and an early Packers lead. (Simmons died in a car accident in 2002. He was only 32.)

Heritage Auction Collection

98 KEN ELLIS, DB*
(PACKER YEARS 1970-75)

Ellis, a cornerback and safety, was a fourth-round draft pick out of Southern University. An All-Pro in '72 and '73, Ellis was part of the trade that sent Lynn Dickey from the Houston Oilers to the Packers. In addition to the Oilers, he played for four other teams, including Super Bowl XIV as a member of the LA Rams. He is an associate pastor at Bethany World Prayer Center.

Card and Coin/Packer City Antiques

97 CHARLIE BROCK, C/LB*
(PACKER YEARS 1939-47)

Brock was a key member of the Packers' 1939 and 1944 championship teams. He is a somewhat surprising omission from the Pro Football Hall of Fame.

Card and Coin/Packer City Antiques

96 MIKE DOUGLASS, LB*
(PACKER YEARS 1978-85)

The undersized Douglass was a standout on some mostly mediocre Packers' defenses. Mike Douglass picked up the nickname "Mad Dog" early in his career for his crazy style of play. He is the third-leading tackler in Packers history.

Mark Forsech Collection

95 GILBERT BROWN, DT*
(PACKER YEARS 1993-99, 01-03)

The Gravedigger, a hefty but talented lineman, plugged the middle (and did a dance) like few Packers before or since. You remember the McDonald's jingle...."Two all-beef patties, special sauce, lettuce, cheese, pickles..." Whoa, stop there. No Big Macs for Gilbert Brown. The Gravedigger was known for his love of double Whoppers from Burger King – but hold the pickles! Following the Packers' Super Bowl XXXI title, Brown turned down a lucrative offer from the Jacksonville Jaguars to remain with the Packers.

Creative Commons

94 BUFORD "BABY" RAY, T*
(PACKER YEARS 1938-48)

A standout at both offensive and defensive tackle, Ray was a large player for his day, standing 6-foot-6, and weighing around 255. He shed the pounds to improve his mobility, which was roughly 25 pounds less than his college playing weight! Ray was a member of the Packers' 1939 and 1944 championship teams. He was named to the NFL 1940s All-Decade Team.

Creative Commons

93 JOSH SITTON, G
(PACKER YEARS 2008-15)

A fourth-round pick out of Central Florida, the recently retired guard made four Pro Bowls during a solid 11-year career. The road-grading guard was a surprising Packers' roster cut just before the start of the 2016 season. He played two seasons for the Chicago Bears before moving on to the Miami Dolphins.

Card and Coin/Packer City Antiques

92 HOWIE FERGUSON, RB*
(PACKER YEARS 1953-58)

Ferguson, who never played college ball, was a free agent signing in 1953. The 6'2", 210-pound Ferguson – a standout on some mediocre (at best) Packers teams – gained 2,120 yards rushing and 1,079 yards receiving with the Packers.

Tony Pruelm Collection

91 JESSE WHITTENTON, CB*
(PACKER YEARS 1958-64)

A starter on the 1961 and '62 championship teams, he paced the team with six interceptions in 1960. A two-time Pro Bowl selection, Whittenton picked Giants' QB Y.A. Tittle in Green Bay's 1961 championship win over New York - the Packers' first title in 17 years!

Mark Forsch Collection

90 FRANK WINTERS, C*
(PACKER YEARS 1992-02)

"Frankie Baggadonuts" was the Packers' starting center for eight straight seasons (1993–2000). Frank Winters – along with teammates Brett Favre and Mark Chmura – was one of the Three Amigos, so named for the trios' close friendship. Winters was a free agent pickup in 1992 – one of the Packers' better moves in free agency over the years.

89-80

GREATEST PACKERS OF ALL TIME

Card and Coin/Packer City Antiques

89 DOUG EVANS, CB
(PACKER YEARS 1993-97)

A sixth-round pick out of Louisiana Tech, Evans's pick-six in a 1996 regular season win over the Rams jump started the Packers from an 8-3 freefall to an eventual title. As well as providing a pivotal play in the regular season, Evans was a solid defender no matter the game. In 1996, he recorded five interceptions and three sacks. Unbelievably, the underrated Evans did not make the Pro Bowl.

Mark Forseth Collection

88 MARK CHMURA, TE*
(PACKER YEARS 1992-99)

A three-time Pro Bowl selection, Chmura scored the final points of Super Bowl XXXI on a 2-point conversion catch. "Chewy", one of Brett Favre's favorite targets, snared 188 passes as one of the leading tight ends in Packers history. In 2000, he was accused, though found not guilty, of sexually assaulting a teenage girl in a hot tub. He was inducted into the team's Hall of Fame in 2010.

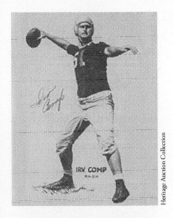

Heritage Auction Collection

87 IRV COMP, BACK*
(PACKER YEARS 1943-49)

A Milwaukee native, Comp still holds the Packers record for most interceptions in a season with 10 in 1943. Irving Henry Comp Jr. played his entire seven-year career with the Packers and was enshrined in the team's Hall of Fame in 1986. He died in 1989 at age 70. Like another Packer whose name will come up much later in this list, Comp could only see out of one eye.

Mark Forsech Collection

86 RON KOSTELNIK, DT*
(PACKER YEARS 1961-68)

An unheralded member of the Packers' vaunted defensive line during the Lombardi years, Kostelnik did the "dirty work" that allowed others to make big plays. He was only 53 when he died in an auto accident in 1993.

Mark Forsech Collection

85 FRED "FUZZY" THURSTON, G*
(PACKER YEARS 1959-67)

Lombardi acquired the Altoona, Wis. native from the Colts. Fuzzy became a two-time All-Pro, who paired with RG Jerry Kramer to lead the vaunted Packers' sweep during the Lombardi championship years. A fan favorite, he owned "Fuzzy's," a bar in Green Bay not far from Lambeau Field.

Tony Prudom Collection

84 HANK GREMMINGER, CB*
(PACKER YEARS 1956-65)

Gremminger played for the Packers for 10 seasons, three of which were championship years ('61, '62 and '65). Charles Henry "Hank" Gremminger, a seventh-round draft pick out of Baylor in 1956, played defensive back for 11 seasons in the NFL. He was named to the Packers Hall of Fame in 1976. Gremminger died in 2001 at age 68.

Card and Coin/Packer City Antiques

83 JOE LAWS, HB*
(PACKER YEARS 1934-1945)

Laws played on three championship teams under Curly Lambeau. In an era when players played both ways, Laws intercepted three passes in the Packers' 14-7 title win over the Giants in '44. He was inducted into the Packers Hall of Fame in 1972.

Card and Coin/Packer City Antiques

82 EZRA JOHNSON, DE*
(PACKER YEARS 1977-87)

While perhaps better known for eating a hot dog on the sidelines during a Packers preseason game, the Packers' number-one draft pick's on-field contributions were significant – including an unofficial 20-1/2 sacks in 1978 and 14-1/2 sacks in 1983. (Sacks were not an official NFL statistic until 1982.)

Heritage Auction Collection

81 JOHNNY HOLLAND, LB*
(PACKER YEARS 1987-93)

Holland, a second-round draft pick in '87, posted 100-plus tackles for six-consecutive years. After his retirement, Holland moved into a coaching career. He was a defensive quality control coach with the Packers from 1995-97, and is presently a linebackers and running game coach with the 49ers. In addition to the Packers Hall of Fame, Holland has also been inducted into the Cotton Bowl and Texas A&M "Halls" (his alma mater).

Card and Coin/Packer City Antiques

80 BRIAN NOBLE, LB
(PACKER YEARS 1985-93)

Often overlooked in team annals, all Noble did was tackle. Four times in his nine-year history in GB, he paced the team in tackles. The steady Noble also had five fumble recoveries in the strike-shortened '87 season. Alas, with a bad knee injury, his career ended just as the Packers were becoming steady winners.

GREATEST PACKERS OF ALL TIME

Creative Commons

79 AARON KAMPMAN, DE/LB
(PACKER YEARS 2002-09)

With 54 career sacks, including 15-1/2 in 2006, it might be just a matter of time before this relentless pass rusher is in the Packers' Hall of Fame. Aaron Kampman was chosen by the Packers with the 21st pick in the fifth round of the 2002 NFL draft. He was a two-time Pro Bowl selection and was twice named the NFL defensive player of the week in 2006. Reggie White is the only other Packers to receive that honor.

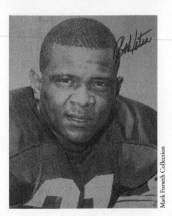

Mark Forsyth Collection

78 BOB JETER, CB*
(PACKER YEARS 1963-70)

A former running back and wide receiver, Jeter was converted to cornerback in '65 and posted 26 career interceptions. He was a two-time Pro Bowler and was inducted into the Packers Hall of Fame in 1985. His son, Rob, was the head coach of the men's basketball team at the University of Wisconsin-Milwaukee.

77 CHARLES "BUCKETS" GOLDENBERG, G/RB*

(PACKER YEARS 1933-45)

Goldenberg was born in Odessa, Ukraine. His family immigrated to Wisconsin in the United States when he was 4 years old. He is not in the NFL HOF even though "Buckets" (a play on "buttocks") was named the "Outstanding Jewish Athlete of All Time" by the Green Bay B'nai B'rith Lodge in 1969.

76 KEN RUETTGERS, OT*

(PACKER YEARS 1985-96)

Ruettgers, a standout left tackle, was a fixture on the Packers' offensive line. Sadly, injuries did not allow him to finish what ended up being a Packers championship season in '96.

75 TIM HARRIS, DE/LB

(PACKER YEARS 1986-90)

Harris talked a lot on the field, but his play backed it up: His 19-1/2 sacks in 1989 remains the club's single-season record. (Ezra Johnson recorded an unofficial 20-1/2 sacks in 1978, but this was before official sack records were kept.) Harris's 55 sacks as a Packer ranks fourth all-time.

Card and Coin/Packer City Antiques

74 MARK MURPHY, S*
(PACKER YEARS 1980-85, 87-91)

It might surprise some to learn the Packers had a player named Mark Murphy – and a pretty darn good one at that – long before there was a Packers' CEO (a different M. Murphy) by the same name. The Packers' player named Murphy led Green Bay in interceptions three times, and paced the team in total tackles twice. Not bad for an undrafted free agent!

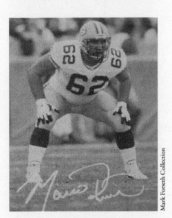

Mark Forsyth Collection

73 MARCO RIVERA, G*
(PACKER YEARS 1997-04)

A sixth-round draft pick out of Penn State, Rivera continued to elevate his game until he became a three-time Pro Bowl selection. He was part of a stalwart '03 group that was often considered one of the Pack's best OLs of all time. Rivera was named to the 2011 class of the Green Bay Packers Hall of Fame.

Creative Commons, Paul Cutler

72 DON MAJKOWSKI, QB*
(PACKER YEARS 1987-92)

While injuries led to a "what-might-have-been?" type career, there is no disputing that Don was "Majik" in 1989, when his 27 touchdowns, and 4,318 passing yards paced the Cardiac Pack to a 10-6 record that just missed a playoff berth. The most notable victory was the famous "instant replay" win over the hated Bears.

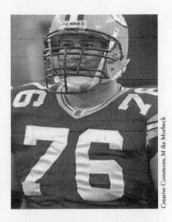

Creative Commons, Mike Morbeck

71 CHAD CLIFTON, OT*
(PACKER YEARS 2000-11)

A second-round draft pick out of Tennessee, Clifton had the good fortune of blocking for three HOF quarterbacks (Peyton Manning in college, and Favre and Rodgers in GB). Protecting the blind side of two legendary Packers signal callers, the left tackle was a two-time Pro Bowler and outstanding pass blocker.

Mark Forseth Collection

70 LEROY CAFFEY, LB*
(PACKER YEARS 1964-69)

Caffey was acquired by the Packers in the famous Jim Ringo trade, and went on to start 80 out of 84 games and named an All-Pro. The Packers' linebacking trio of Nitschke, Robinson, and Caffey was often considered the best in the game. Did you know that Caffey made some important plays in the famous Ice Bowl? In the third quarter, he forced a fumble that was recovered by Herb Adderley to thwart one Cowboys' drive. Later in the same stanza, he sacked Dallas QB Don Meredith on a nine-yard loss that forced a field goal attempt that fell short. Sadly, he died of colon cancer at the young age of 52

69-60
GREATEST PACKERS OF ALL TIME

Wikimedia Commons

69 TED FRITSCH, FB*
(PACKER YEARS 1942-50)

A devastating blocker, Fritsch was named All-Pro in 1944, '45, and '46. He scored both touchdowns in Green Bay's 1944 championship win over the Giants. A Stevens Point grad, Fritsch led the Packers in scoring six times, which still ranks 12th in team history.

Mark Forsecht Collection

68 ROBERT BROOKS, WR*
(PACKER YEARS 1992-98)

A third-round pick out of South Carolina, Brooks really came into his own in '95, following a career-ending injury to Sterling Sharpe. His 102-catch, 13 TD, 1,497 receiving yards in '95 included a 99-yard hookup with Favre against the Bears. Brooks, a fan favorite, also popularized the Lambeau Leap.

Card and Coin/Packer City Antiques

67 RICH McGEORGE, TE
(PACKER YEARS 1970-78)

A first-round pick out of tiny Elon College, McGeorge is one of the Packers' most underrated players of all time. A good blocker and reliable receiver, his stats weren't stellar, but that's due to two reasons: the Packers ran the ball more than they threw it back then, and GB's quarterbacks at the time were a pedestrian bunch.

Creative Commons

66 RYAN GRANT, RB
(PACKER YEARS 2007-2012)

It might surprise some to learn that Grant is the Pack's 5th leading rusher all-time, just behind the legendary Tony Canadeo. Picked up by Ted Thompson in '07 when Green Bay was in dire need of a running back, Grant amassed 956 yards on an excellent 5.1 average. His top season was a 1,253-yard campaign in '09. But he had to watch Super Bowl XLV from the sidelines, as he had a season-ending ankle injury.

Card and Coin/Packer City Antiques

65 JOHNNIE GRAY, S*
(PACKER YEARS 1975-83)

Signed as a free agent out of Cal-Fullerton, the hard-hitting Gray led the team in tackles his rookie season. Equally adept against the pass, he also paced the team in interceptions three times. It's easy to overlook that as well as a talented safety, Johnnie Gray was also a skilled punt and kickoff returner. He was named to the team's Hall of Fame in 1993.

Wikimedia Commons

64 BILLY HOWTON, WR*
(PACKER YEARS 1952-58)

Howton is one of the best Packers receivers of all time, but he isn't that well known because he had the misfortune of playing on some poor teams in the '50s just before Lombardi's arrival. His 303 catches still ranks 16th all-time – and his 18.4 average per catch is only exceeded by Carroll Dale.

Mark Forsch Collection

63 CARROLL DALE, WR*
(PACKER YEARS 1965-72)

Obtained in a trade with the Rams for Packers' LB Dan Currie, the swift Dale was an integral receiver on three championship teams. His 275 catches ranks just behind Howton, and his blistering 19.7 average per catch is tops in team annals. J.J. Kelly High School in his home state of Virginia was named "Carroll Dale Stadium" in his honor.

Creative Commons

62 WILLIAM HENDERSON, FB*
(PACKER YEARS 1995-06)

A third-round pick out of North Carolina in 1995, Henderson was just as home circling out of the backfield to catch a pass, as he was "pancaking" a blitzing linebacker. His 320 grabs rank 14th all-time, and second among running backs. "Old Reliable" as he was called, played in 188 games in the Green and Gold, 5th most all-time.

Creative Commons, Mike Morbeck

61 JAMES JONES, WR
(PACKER YEARS 2007-13, 15)

A third-round draft pick out of San Jose State in '07, Jones was a starter his rookie season. His 14 touchdowns in 2012 led the NFL. Jones's 360 catches ranks 10th in team annals. James Jones is currently working as an analyst on the NFL Network. With the exception of a one-year stop in Oakland, he played his entire career in Green Bay.

Mark Forseth Collection

60 LAVVIE DILWEG, END*
(PACKER YEARS 1927-34)

Dilweg was an outstanding offensive end and a solid tackler on defense. (Offensive ends were precursors to today's wide receivers.) Dilweg was considered the best all-around end in football before Don Hutson. A star on the Packers' first three championship teams, he was a member of the NFL All-Decade Team of the 1920s. His grandson, Anthony Dilweg, played quarterback for the Packers. Dilweg, a lawyer, served briefly in Congress in the 1940s.

59-50
GREATEST PACKERS OF ALL TIME

Creative Commons, Keith Allison

59 RANDALL COBB, WR
(PACKER YEARS 2011–)

Not many players break onto the scene the way Cobb did, as he broke a Packers' record with a 108-yard kickoff return in 2011 against the Saints. Plus of course not one, but two game-winners against the Bears! Cobb ranks seventh in pass receptions in team annals. Pretty impressive for an 8-year Packers career in which the standout slot receiver was often injured.

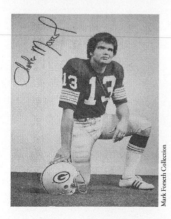

Mark Forseth Collection

58 CHESTER MARCOL, K*
(PACKER YEARS 1972-80)

Marcol lived in Poland until age 14, when his father committed suicide, forcing his mother to relocate to the United States - where they settled in Michigan. He attended tiny Hillsdale College, where his kicking caught the attention of pro scouts, including the Packers. As a rookie, he drilled 33 field goals in '72, a season-high number that remains tied for first in team history. Who could ever forget him grabbing a blocked kick that bounced back at him, and running in for a touchdown against the Bears in 1980? But perhaps Marcol's greatest feat was his post-NFL comeback from drug and alcohol addiction.

Mark Forseth Collection

57 RON KRAMER, TE*
(PACKER YEARS 1957, 59-64)

Kramer was one of the first outstanding tight ends in the NFL. Kramer, an integral member of Lombardi's early championship years, caught 37 passes and 7 TDs in '62, good enough to be named to the Pro Bowl. In 1965, he asked to be traded to the Lions to be closer to his wife and family.

Card and Coin/Packer City Antiques

56 GERRY ELLIS, RB*
(PACKER YEARS 1980-86)

Ellis, a feared dual threat, could run AND catch. His versatility helped him snare 267 passes (19th in team history), and 3,826 rushing yards, which ranks 8th. The Packers of that period made their mark more through the air than on the ground, but Ellis's abilities helped keep defenses honest.

Heritage Auction Collection

55 JOHN ANDERSON, LB*
(PACKER YEARS 1978-89)

John Anderson was the second of the Packers' two first-round draft picks in 1978 (the first being James Lofton). An All-American at Michigan, his Packers career got off to a rough start when he broke his arm in his first two seasons. After those injuries, Anderson went on to start in 140 games and was named the Packers' defensive MVP three times. Anderson retired from the Packers as the team's all-time leader in tackles, and was tied with Ray Nitschke for the Packers' career interception leader for a linebacker.

Mark Forsch Collection

54 EDGAR BENNETT, RB*
(PACKER YEARS 1992-96)

Bennett was a fourth-round draft pick out of Florida State. He started his Packers career as a fullback, but he became a starting RB in '95 and topped 1,000 yards rushing. Like Gerry Ellis, Bennett was an excellent receiver. Bennett, a reliable runner who rarely fumbled, even in lousy late-season GB weather, ranks 11th as a Packers rusher. Bennett was a coach with the Packers from 2005-2017, and is presently with the Oakland Raiders.

Mark Forsch Collection

53 PAUL COFFMAN, TE*
(PACKER YEARS 1978-85)

Few tight ends have a made a bigger contribution than Coffman did as one of the NFL's premier TEs. Undrafted out of Kansas State, Coffman was a three-time Pro Bowl TE on some of the highest-scoring offenses in Packers history. Paul Coffman caught 56 passes in 1979, breaking Ron Kramer's team record. He scored two TDs in the Packers' 48-47 win over Washington in 1983. His son, Chase, was a standout TE at Missouri.

52 MAX McGEE, WR*
(PACKER YEARS 1954, 57-67)

The colorful McGee was often at his best in the biggest games. He famously caught seven passes, two of which went for TDs, in Green Bay's 35-10 win over Kansas City in the first Super Bowl. He was also an accomplished punter. (His 41.6-yd gross average still ranks fifth in team annals.)

Mark Forseth Collection

51 VERN LEWELLEN, BACK/P*
(PACKER YEARS 1924-32)

Lewellen was a star on Curly Lambeau's early championship teams. Since statistical records from that era are lacking, it is easy to overlook his importance in Packers' lore. Following his football career, Lewellen became an attorney and practiced law until his retirement. He even served as the Packers' general manager from 1954-58. He was elected to the team's Hall of Fame in 1970.

Mark Forseth Collection

50 CHRIS JACKE, K*
(PACKER YEARS 1989-96)

Jacke was never a stranger to pressure kicks during his Packers' career, as his timely boots helped lead the Pack to a 10-6 record in '89. None were more dramatic than his 53-yard field goal in overtime that downed the 49ers on Monday night in '96. He retired as the Packers' fourth-leading scorer, just behind legendary flanker Don Hutson.

49-40

GREATEST PACKERS OF ALL TIME

Card and Coin/Packer City Antiques

49 DORSEY LEVENS, RB*
(PACKER YEARS 1994-01)

Levens burst on the scene in the '97 NFC Championship game against Carolina with 88 yards rushing, and 117 yards receiving (and a touchdown). The next year, following a preseason injury to Edgar Bennett, Levens rambled for 1,435 yards, just missing Jim Taylor's single-season Packers' record. He is the sixth-leading Packers rusher of all time.

Wikimedia Commons

48 TOBIN ROTE, QB*
(PACKER YEARS 1950-56)

A talented runner as well as passer, Rote led the Packers in rushing three times and rushing touchdowns five times. In 1956, Rote amassed an amazing 29 touchdowns, 18 via the air and 11 on the ground. The Detroit Lions acquired Rote from the Packers prior to the 1957 season. Rote, filling in for an injured Bobby Layne, led the Lions to the '57 title - their last championship!

Card and Coin/Packer City Antiques

47 KABEER GBAJA-BIAMILA, DE*
(PACKER YEARS 2000-08)

"KGB" was one of the top sack artists in Packers history, totaling 74-1/2 sacks, a team record since broken by Clay Matthews. In 2003, the swift DE became the first player in Packers history to record 10 or more sacks in three consecutive seasons.

Creative Commons, Gabriel Cervantes

46 GREG JENNINGS, WR
(PACKER YEARS 2006-12)

Jennings, another of Ted Thompson's WR gems, was a second-round selection out of Western Michigan in 2006. Jennings made a LOT of big plays during his Packers' career, which included hauling in four passes for 64 yards and two scores in the Packers' 31-25 Super Bowl XLV win over the Pittsburgh Steelers. His 425 catches rank 9th all-time in Packer annals. And few can say they caught touchdown passes from Brett Favre AND Aaron Rodgers!

Creative Commons, cropped

45 LARRY McCARREN, C*
(PACKER YEARS 1973-84)

Much better known today as a TV broadcaster and radio analyst, it might surprise some to learn that McCarren was a two-time Pro Bowler. He earned the nickname "The Rock" after starting in 162 consecutive games, one of the longest such streaks in team annals.

Card and Coin/Packer City Antiques

44 MARK LEE, CB*
(PACKER YEARS 1980-90)

Lee played on some mostly crummy Packers teams, but his contributions shouldn't be overlooked. He recorded 31 interceptions, including a career-high nine in '86, which remains tied for second in Packers' history. The steady Mark Lee was selected for the Packers' Hall of Fame in 2017.

Creative Commons

43 NICK COLLINS, S*
(PACKER YEARS 2005-11)

Collins, a two-time Pro Bowler, cemented his place in Packers' lore with a pick-six that helped pace the Packers to a 31-25 victory over the Steelers in SB XLV. He suffered a season-ending neck injury against Carolina in 2011, and that sadly was the end of his playing career.

Card and Coin/Packer City Antiques

42 CECIL ISBELL, TB/QB*
(PACKER YEARS 1938-42)

He alternated with Arnie Herber early in his career, but eventually blossomed as a passer in his own right. His streak of 23-straight games with a TD pass from '40-'42, was a league record until broken by Johnny Unitas in '57. Also in 1942, Don Hutson caught 74 of Isbell's passes for 1,211 yards and 17 touchdowns.

Mark Forseth Collection

41 BOB SKORONSKI, OT*
(PACKER YEARS 1956, 59-68)

No less than Bart Starr sang Skoronski's praises, lauding
"Ski" as an elite tackle, and deserving of NFL HOF
status. Skoronski was an offensive captain on five Packers
championship teams.

Mark Forseth Collection

40 ANTONIO FREEMAN, WR*
(PACKER YEARS 1995-01, 03)

Freeman, out of Virginia Tech, was one of three 3rd-
round draft picks by Ron Wolf in 1995. (The others were
William Henderson and Brian Williams.) Freeman led the
Packers in receiving from 1996–1999, and led the NFL
in receiving in 1998 (84 passes for 1,424 yards). Many
of Freeman's grabs made highlight reels, including his
81-yard hookup with Brett Favre in Super Bowl XXXI,
and his unbelievable game-winning OT TD against the
Vikings in 2000.

39-30
GREATEST PACKERS OF ALL TIME

Mark Forsch Collection

39 GALE GILLINGHAM, G*
(PACKER YEARS 1966-74, 76)

Noted for his impressive strength, Gilly, a starter in the Ice Bowl, was a five-time Pro Bowler and six-time All-Pro. He died at age 67, in 2011, in Little Falls, Minnesota.

Creative Commons

38 RYAN LONGWELL, K*
(PACKER YEARS 1997-05)

Longwell became the Packers' all-time leading scorer before leaving for Minnesota in free agency. (He still ranks second behind Crosby.) He is one of just three Packers kickers to boot 33 field goals in a single season. Longwell's Packers highlights include four game-winners in the 2004 season, featuring a FG to win the division against the Vikings on Christmas Eve. Ironically, as noted, he later played for the Vikings.

Card and Coin/Packer City Antiques

37 FRED CARR, LB*
(PACKER YEARS 1968-77)

Carr – a standout in college at University of Texas-EL Paso (UTEP) — was a three-time Pro Bowler on some very mediocre Packers teams. Carr died from prostate cancer and dementia in 2018. He was 71.

Packerland Pride Photo, Rich Palzewic

36 MASON CROSBY, K
(PACKER YEARS 2007-)

The strong-legged Crosby is the Packers' all-time leading scorer, and a surefire future Packers HOFer. He has booted fifty FGs more than any other kicker in Packers' history. With records like these, it's no wonder Crosby has been able to remain the Packers' kicker in spite of several slumps over the years.

Heritage Auction Collection

35 WILLIE BUCHANON, CB*
(PACKER YEARS 1972-78)

Buchanon was the seventh-overall selection in the 1972 draft, and the Defensive Rookie of the Year. Buchanon, a two-time Pro Bowler, led the NFC with 9 interceptions in '78, including four against the Chargers. This tied the NFL record for most interceptions in a single game.

Packerland Pride Photo, Rich Palzewic

34 CLAY MATTHEWS, LB
(PACKER YEARS 2009–)

One of the shrewdest moves Ted Thompson ever made as GM was moving back into the first round to select Matthews with the 26th overall pick in '09. He is the Packers' all-time sacks leader. Clay Matthews III, a six-time Pro Bowler, is the son of former NFL linebacker Clay Matthews Jr., and the nephew of NFL Hall of Fame offensive lineman Bruce Matthews. Thanks for the memories Clay, and good luck with the Rams.

Mark Forseth Collection

33 BOYD DOWLER, WR/P*
(PACKER YEARS 1959-69)

A large receiver for his day (6-5, 220), Dowler caught a pair of TDs in the Ice Bowl and Super Bowl II and was a member of the 1960s All-Decade Team. His 448 receptions still ranks sixth in team annals.

Mark Forseth Collection

32 LYNN DICKEY, QB*
(PACKER YEARS 1976-77, 79-85)

Dickey, acquired from the Houston Oilers in 1976, would soon become a deadly pass-catch duo with star Packers WR James Lofton. Larry McCarren used to say Dickey was the best long-ball thrower he had ever seen. Indeed – his 4,458 yards passing in '83 was the most in team history — until topped by Aaron Rodgers in 2011.

Heritage Auction Collection

31 JOHN BROCKINGTON, RB*
(PACKER YEARS 1971-77)

Exceeding 1,000 yards in each of his first three seasons, few RBs burst on the NFL scene better than the bulldozing Brockington. Brockington remains the Packers' third all-time leading rusher. After receiving a kidney transplant from his future wife, Diane Scott, John Brockington and Diane established the John Brockington Foundation in 2002, to assist others suffering from kidney disease.

Packerland Pride Photo, Rich Palzewic

30 JORDY NELSON, WR
(PACKER YEARS 2008-17)

Nelson, a second-round draft pick out of Kansas State in 2008 – was another of Ted Thompson's terrific draft finds at WR, and quite possibly the best of the bunch. Jordy will go down in Packers' lore as not only of its most popular players, but also one of the best. His 55 catches ranks third all-time in team annals, and his 69 touchdowns as a Packer is third, behind only Don Hutson and Jim Taylor. His 15 TDs in 2011 has only been topped by four other Packers. Overlooked fact: Nelson scored the first touchdown in Super Bowl XLV. As this book went to press, speculation was that Jordy would sign a one-day contract so he could officially retire as a Packer.

29-20
GREATEST PACKERS OF ALL TIME

Card and Coin/Packer City Antiques

29 ARNIE HERBER, QB**
(PACKER YEARS 1930-40)

Herber, a Green Bay native, helped lead the Packers to championships in 1930, '31, '36 and '39. He led the NFL in passing three times and was one of the first great "long-ball" throwers in the league.

Card and Coin/Packer City Antiques

28 DONALD DRIVER, WR*
(PACKER YEARS 1999-12)

Driver, a true rags-to-riches story and a fan favorite, retired as the Packers' all-time leader in pass receptions (743) and receiving yards (10,137). The consistent Driver topped 1,000 receiving yards seven times. "Not bad" for a seventh-round draft pick! Donald Driver, who grew up poor and sometimes lived out of a car, was nicknamed "Quickie" for his prowess in stealing cars. Driver later wrote a number of "Quickie" children's books, including "Quickie Makes the Team" and "Quickie Handles a Loss."

Mark Forseth Collection

27 BOBBY DILLON, DB*
(PACKER YEARS 1952-59)

Nearly sixty years after his retirement, Dillon remains the team's all-time interception leader (52). His total includes nine picks in three different seasons. And, he only had one working eye!

Card and Coin/Packer City Antiques

26 AHMAN GREEN, RB*
(PACKER YEARS 2000-06, 09)

GM Ron Wolf fleeced Seahawks GM Mike Holmgren when he acquired the fumble-prone Green from Seattle for defensive back Fred Vinson. Not quite as big as Wolf's trade for Brett Favre, certainly, but not too far from it. Green is the Packers' all-time leading rusher and he also holds Packers' records for most rushing yards in a single game (218 vs. Denver in '03) and in a single season (1,883 – also in 2003).

Mark Forseth Collection

25 STERLING SHARPE, WR*
(PACKER YEARS 1988-94)

Sharpe had a brilliant seven-year career, setting (then) league records with 108 receptions in '92 and 112 in '93. A neck injury at the end of '94 forced him to retire; a sad end to a tremendous career.

Mark Forsch Collection

24 LEROY BUTLER, S*
(PACKER YEARS 1990-2001)

Did you know that Butler is a real-life Forrest Gump? Challenged by physical problems as a youth, Butler was forced to wear a leg brace and even used a wheelchair while undergoing therapy. Butler is credited with inventing the now-famous Lambeau Leap in a win over the Raiders in '93. Butler recorded 38 INTs, but was also an effective blitzer with 20-1/2 career sacks.

Mark Forsch Collection

23 JIM RINGO, C**
(PACKER YEARS 1953-63)

Although undersized for a center, his outstanding mobility and technique made him an ideal blocker for Lombardi's famous Packers sweep. He was traded to the Eagles for LB Lee Roy Caffey in '64.

Mark Forsch Collection

22 DAVE ROBINSON, LB**
(PACKER YEARS 1963-72)

A first-round draft pick in '63, "Robby" is perhaps best known for preserving the 1966 NFL Championship game over Dallas by pressuring Cowboys' QB Don Meredith into a desperation pass that was intercepted by GB safety Tom Brown.

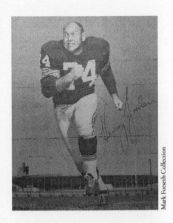

Mark Forseth Collection

21 HENRY JORDAN, DT**
(PACKER YEARS 1959-69)

Jordan, a fiery competitor, was a seven-time All-Pro and Pro Bowl MVP in '61. After retirement, Jordan moved to Milwaukee, where he created Summerfest. He died of a heart attack at age 42 in 1977.

Mark Forseth Collection

20 JAMES LOFTON, WR**
(PACKER YEARS 1978-86)

Lofton, the 6th-overall pick of the 1978 draft, was an NCAA long-jump champion at Stanford. Lofton was an eight-time Pro Bowl pick (seven with Packers, one with the Bills). His 9,656 receiving yards rank second (behind Donald Driver). Always a deep threat, Lofton averaged an amazing 18.2 yards a catch.

19-11

GREATEST PACKERS OF ALL TIME

Card and Coin/Packer City Antiques

19   AUGUST "MIKE" MICHALSKE, G**
(PACKER YEARS 1929-35, 37)

Michalske, also known as "Iron Mike," was inducted into the Pro Football Hall of Fame as part of its second induction class in 1964. Iron Mike led the Packers to three consecutive NFL titles from 1929 to 1931, and was chosen seven times as a first-team All-Pro.

Card and Coin/Packer City Antiques

18   CHARLES WOODSON, CB/S
(PACKER YEARS 2006-12)

Woodson, who elected not to return to the Oakland Raiders, was undoubtedly the leading free agent acquisition of the Ted Thompson era. He was the 2009 Defensive Player of the Year and led the league twice in interceptions ('09 and 2011). The former Heisman Trophy winner out of Michigan had a knack for reading a quarterback's eyes and jumping routes for pick-sixes. He had 65 career interceptions and 13 defensive touchdowns (Packers and Raiders). Undoubtedly a future Packer and NFL HOFer.

Mark Forseth Collection

17   JERRY KRAMER, G**
(PACKER YEARS 1958-68)

While best known for his block on Jethro Pugh that sprung Bart Starr on a QB sneak to win the Ice Bowl, the truth is that such blocks weren't unusual: Kramer was probably the best right guard in the '60s, and of the best ever. Kramer, a five-time First-Team All Pro, was elected to the Pro Football Hall of Fame in 2018. *Finally.*

Mark Forseth Collection

16   WILLIE WOOD, S**
(PACKER YEARS 1960-71)

An undrafted QB out of USC, Wood wrote every team a letter asking for a chance to try out. Only Lombardi responded. Wood asked to be switched to defense, and he was recast as a free safety. Wood, a fierce tackler, was an eight-time Pro Bowler and intercepted 48 passes in his career, second most in Packers history. Playing in an era before specialists, Wood even doubled as a solid punt returner.

Mark Forseth Collection

15   WILLIE DAVIS, DE**
(PACKER YEARS 1960-69)

Davis played in an era when neither tackles nor sacks were official statistics... However, researchers estimate he had more than 100 sacks. Davis, who anchored the Packers' defensive line, was selected five times for the Pro Bowl and as an All-Pro. He played in 138 consecutive games and started in the first two Super Bowls. The shrewd Lombardi obtained Willie Davis in a trade with Cleveland in 1960. The Packers held a "Willie Davis Day" upon his retirement in 1969.

Creative Commons

14 ROBERT "CAL" HUBBARD, T**
(PACKER YEARS 1929-33, 35)

At 6-2, 253, Hubbard was a large player for his day, although he had exceptional quickness for a man his size. Playing "off tackle" as well as on the line, he is considered one of the first NFL linebackers. Hubbard is a member of the NFL 75th Anniversary All-Team and a charter member of the NFL HOF ('63). He later became a MLB umpire and is the only person in the Pro Football HOF and the Baseball Hall of Fame.

Mark Forseth Collection

13 JIM TAYLOR, RB**
(PACKER YEARS 1958-66)

As tough a football player who ever lived, Taylor would rather run through you than around you. He could also take a licking and keep on ticking, which he did in rushing for 85 yards in the Packers' 16-7 title win over the Giants in '62. His top season was a league-leading 1,474 yards and 19 scores that same season. A five-time Pro Bowler, the late Taylor held the Packers' career rushing record for more than 40 years.

Card and Coin/Packer City Antiques

12 JOHNNY "BLOOD" MCNALLY, HALFBACK**

(PACKER YEARS 1929-33, 35-36)

John Victor McNally, better known as Johnny Blood, picked up his famous moniker after watching the movie Blood and Sand starring Rudolph Valentino. Johnny Blood, known for his speed and agility, was an integral part of four championship Packers' teams. He is a charter member of the Pro Football Hall of Fame.

Mark Forsch Collection

11 HERB ADDERLEY, CB**
(PACKER YEARS 1961-69)

Teams ran the ball more than they passed in the '60s, but a dominant defense still needed an elite cover corner, and Adderley was just that. Adderley, a four-time First-Team All-Pro, started in the first two Super Bowls, which included a pick-six against the Raiders in SB II. He is one of a handful of players to play on six championship teams.

TOP 10
GREATEST PACKERS OF ALL TIME

Heritage Auction Collection

10 CLARKE HINKLE, FB/LB**
(PACKER YEARS 1932-41)

Hinkle, a seven-time First-Team All-Pro, had both power and speed. In 1937, he led the NFL with seven touchdowns and finished second with 552 rushing yards. He also led the league in scoring in '38. More than 75 years since he retired, Hinkle is still GB's seventh-leading rusher all-time. In 1997, the Packers' practice field on Oneida Avenue across from Lambeau Field was dedicated as "Clarke Hinkle Field." The bruising Hinkle, an extremely tough runner and tackler, was reportedly the only player to knock out Bears great Bronko Nagurski in an NFL contest.

A CENTURY OF EXCELLENCE

Mark Forsch Collection

9   PAUL HORNUNG, HB**
(PACKER YEARS 1957-62, 64-66)

The "Golden Boy" was a true money player, always at his best in the biggest games. In 1960, the versatile Hornung scored an incredible 176 points on 15 FGs, 15 touchdowns, and 41 PATs. And this was in a 12-game season! The record wasn't broken until 2006 (by LaDainian Tomlinson). He was also the league's MVP in 1961 and rushed for five touchdowns in a 1965 game against the Colts.

Mark Forsch Collection

8   TONY CANADEO, HB***
(PACKER YEARS 1941-44, 46-52)

The "Gray Ghost of Gonzaga", a nickname he picked up in college, was a triple-threat halfback, leading the team in rushing and passing in '43. After serving in the Army in World War II, Canadeo primarily served as a RB, and in '49 became just the third player in NFL history to top 1,000 yards rushing. Canadeo retired as the Packers' all-time rushing leader, and still ranks fourth in team annals. His "3" is one of just six numbers retired by the team. After his playing career, Canadeo was a longtime member of the Packers' Executive Committee.

Mark Forsch Collection

7 REGGIE WHITE, DE***
(PACKER YEARS 1993-98)

White left the Philadelphia Eagles to become THE free agent signing of '93. The Minister of Defense was a two-time NFL Defensive Player of the Year, and 13-time Pro Bowl, and All-Pro selection. White holds second place all-time among career sack leaders with 198 (68.5 as a Packer). He was also just as valued for his role as a team leader. White's former college (Tennessee), and NFL teams (Eagles) and Packers all retired his "92". White left us much too soon - dying on December 26, 2004, at age 43.

Mark Forsch Collection

6 RAY NITSCHKE, LB***
(PACKER YEARS 1958-72)

While not as decorated as some of his teammates of that era (one Pro Bowl selection?) there's no question Nitschke was the heart and soul of the Packers' formidable defenses of the '60s. He recovered two fumbles, and deflected a pass (that was picked off) in the '62 championship against the Giants. (He was the game's MVP as result.) Nitschke was known as a fierce tackler, but the agile LB also intercepted 25 passes in his career. Opening in 2009, "Ray Nitschke Field" has been a tremendous addition to Packers' training camps. He died of a heart attack at age 61 in 1998.

Card and Coin/Packer City Antiques

5   FORREST GREGG, OT**
(PACKER YEARS 1956, 58-70)

Long before Brett Favre, Gregg was another 'iron man,'
playing in 188 consecutive games. He was selected to play
in nine Pro Bowls and was a seven-time First-Team All-Pro.
Like teammate Herb Adderley, Gregg joined the Cowboys
for a final season, helping them win Super Bowl VI. No
less than Vince Lombardi called him, "the finest player I
ever coached." A key reason he is rated this high on this
list. Who am I to doubt Vince?

Packerland Pride Photo, Rich Palzewic

4   AARON RODGERS, QB
(PACKER YEARS 2005-)

A-Rod could well wind up even higher in a future list of
this sort, but with his stellar career still a work in progress,
this spot seems about right for the two-time league MVP,
and Super Bowl XLV MVP. So far, his Packers passing
records include highest passer rating career (103.8),
highest passer rating season (122.5, 2011), most passes
completed season (401, 2016), and most yards passing
season (4,643, 2011). And that's not even including his
Hail Mary's!

Mark Forsch Collection

3   BRETT FAVRE, QB***
(PACKER YEARS 1992-07)

I've always said, Favre might not be the best QB of all time, but he was definitely the most entertaining! At the time of his retirement, the three-time league MVP ('95-'97) and 11-time Pro Bowler held virtually every major NFL passing record. Known as the "gunslinger" due to his penchant for costly interceptions, it seems Favre was either very bad, or very good, and sometimes in the same game! But when he was ON, no one was better.

Mark Forsch Collection

2   BART STARR, QB***
(PACKER YEARS 1956-71)

Does one grade all-time great quarterbacks by outstanding career statistics? The number of championships? I lean toward the latter, hence my ranking of Starr ahead of Rodgers and Favre. While lacking Favre's and Rodgers's athletic abilities, Starr never wavered in big games. If Hornung was "money" in big games, then Bart Starr was gold. The Packers were 9-1 in playoff games under his direction, with Starr completing 61 percent of his passes in those games, with 15 touchdowns and just three interceptions. As Hornung and Taylor aged, Starr assumed a larger role in the passing game. In '66, he was First-Team All-Pro and league MVP. His passer rating that year was 108.3, impressive even by today's standards. Starr was also an excellent play caller, and he once threw 294 passes without an INT.

Photo courtesy of Green Bay Packers

1

DON HUTSON, SPLIT END***
(PACKER YEARS 1935-45)

Precious few players revolutionize a position, but the "Alabama Antelope" did just that. Hutson was from Alabama. A standout pass catcher and route runner when running the ball was far more popular, Hutson's stats – which included 74 pass receptions for 1,211 yards in '42 – were unheard of at the time. In a blowout win over the Lions in '45, Hutson scored an incredible 29 points in a single quarter, which remains a league record. Hutson's single season record of 17 touchdown receptions in 1942 stood for 42 years until broken by Mark Clayton in '84. More than 70 years since his retirement, his 105 career TDs remains a Packers record.

HONORABLE MENTION

* Asterisk indicates player is in Packers Hall Of Fame

A.J. HAWK, LB (PACKER YEARS 2006-14)

Hawk never met the lofty standards that come with being the fifth overall selection in the 2006 draft, but the steady Hawk led the team in tackles in five of his nine seasons in Green Bay.

BUBBA FRANKS, TE (PACKER YEARS 2000-07)

In dire need of a tight end following the departure of Mark Chmura, Franks the first-round draft pick out of the University of Miami delivered. The unspectacular, though steady Franks was a three-time Pro Bowler and caught a career-high nine TD passes in 2001.

SAM SHIELDS, CB (PACKER YEARS 2010-16)

The speedy Shields had a solid career for an undrafted DB who started out as a WR at the University of Miami. After sitting out of the 2017 season following a series of concussions, he recently resurrected his career with the LA Rams.

DONNY ANDERSON, RB/P* (PACKER YEARS 1966-71)

Anderson is the Packers' 12th-all-time rusher, ranking just behind Eddie Lacy and Edgar Bennett in team annals. Anderson made several key plays in the game-winning drive in the Ice Bowl, and he scored a touchdown in Super Bowl II.

EDDIE LACY, RB (PACKER YEARS 2013-16)

What might have been? The hard-running Lacy, known for an effective spin move, began his Packers' career with back-to-back 1,000+ seasons, but injuries robbed him of his effectiveness after that.

BILL FORESTER, LB* (PACKER YEARS 1953-63)

Forester was a five-time All-Pro, played in four Pro Bowls, and he was a defensive captain. A tough scratch from the top 100 list.

DAVANTE ADAMS, WR (PACKER YEARS 2014-)

Where would the Packers' offense have been in 2018 if not for Adams? With a larger body of work, Adams would easily crack a future list of 100 all-time Packers. He just missed this one.

BRYCE PAUP, LB (PACKER YEARS 1990-94)

Did the Packers make a mistake letting Paup leave in free agency? He was the NFL Defensive Player of the Year in his first year with the Bills in '95, so you be the judge.

DAN CURRIE, LB* (PACKER YEARS 1958-64)

Currie was the #1 pick in Green Bay's loaded 1958 draft that also produced Hall of Famers Jim Taylor (round 2), Ray Nitschke (#3) and Jerry Kramer (#4). After seven years with the Packers, Currie was traded to the Rams for WR Carroll Dale in 1965.

FRED CONE, FB/K* (PACKER YEARS 1951-57)

Cone is one of the Packers who played during the miserable, losing '50s, which has undoubtedly cost him some accolades over the years. That he still ranks eighth in team scoring all time is a testament to his play.

HALL OF FAMERS WORTH MENTIONING

The majority of the Packers enshrined in Canton played most – if not all – of their careers in Green Bay. Bart Starr, Paul Hornung, and Jerry Kramer are among those who come to mind.

Then there are players who suited up not only with the Packers but also before that (or afterward) with other teams. Think players like Reggie White (Eagles) and James Lofton (Raiders, Bills).

But there are a precious few who stopped in Titletown only briefly on their way to enshrinement in Canton. Most notably, those players are:

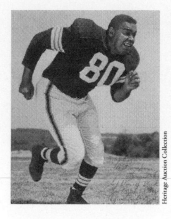

Heritage Auction Collection

LEN FORD, DE

(Posthumously enshrined in Canton in 1976).

1948-49 Los Angeles Dons (All-America Football Conference)
1950-57 Cleveland Browns
1958 Green Bay Packers

Ford began his career with the Dons of the old AAFC – no small feat considering how few African-Americans were playing professional sports back then.

Cleveland claimed Ford when the Dons (and AAFC) disbanded, with Head Coach Paul Brown converting him to defensive end. Ford was a defensive stalwart on talented Browns teams of the 1950s.

He was traded to Green Bay in '58 .... a 1-10-1 debacle that Ford, and the rest of the Packers would just as soon forget.

Card and Coin/Packer City Antiques

WALT KIESLING, G
(Posthumously enshrined in Canton in 1966).

1926-27 Duluth Eskimos
1928 Pottsville Maroons
1929-1933 Chicago Cardinals
1934 Chicago Bears
1935-36 Green Bay Packers
1937-38 Pittsburgh Pirates

At 6-3, 260, Kiesling was a large player for his day. A well-conditioned athlete and solid tackler, Kiesling was a member of Green Bay's 1936 championship team.

Creative Commons

TED HENDRICKS, LB
(Enshrined in Canton in 1990).

1969-73 Baltimore Colts
1974 Green Bay Packers
1975-83 Oakland / LA Raiders

After five seasons in Baltimore, Hendricks was traded to the Packers, where the All-Pro put together another solid campaign with five interceptions and seven blocked kicks. The 6-7 Hendricks had a penchant for knocking down passes and blocking kicks throughout his stellar career.

In a downtrodden Packers era in which great players like Hendricks were few and far between, Green Bay was criticized for allowing Raiders owner Al Davis to sign him. The Packers did receive a pair of first-round draft picks for the talented linebacker, but was that enough? Some would say no.

Mark Forseth Collection

JAN STENERUD, K

(Enshrined in Canton in 1991)

1967-79 Kansas City Chiefs
1980-83 Green Bay Packers
1984-85 Minnesota Vikings

One of the first "soccer style" placekickers, the Norwegian-born Stenerud was a highly accurate kicker in an era when kickers more typically made only a little better than 50 percent of field goal tries.

With the Packers in the midst of kicking woes, Coach Bart Starr was more than happy to snap up Stenerud from the Chiefs and resolve their kicking situation. Stenerud is one of just five kickers in the Pro Football HOF. His No. "3" is retired by the Chiefs. (He has been inducted in both Chiefs and Packers "Halls.")

Card and Coin/Packer City Antiques

EMLEN TUNNELL, DB

(Enshrined in Canton in 1967)

1948-58 New York Giants
1959-61 Green Bay Packers

Tunnell was a standout punt returner and defensive back on some talented Giants teams of that era. He played in eight Pro Bowls and intercepted 74 passes – a Giants record that still stands – all the more remarkable when you consider that teams only played 12-game schedules back then, and threw the ball considerably less than they do today.

New Packers Coach Vince Lombardi shrewdly traded for the talented Tunnell. He was not as good as he once was, but the experienced DB was still plenty good enough to help "coach" Green Bay's young defensive players.

PLAYER NICKNAMES

PACKERS WITH LEGENDARY MONIKERS

MIKE "MAD DOG" DOUGLASS

PAUL "GOLDEN BOY" HORNUNG

CHARLES "BUCKETS" GOLDENBERG

FRED "FUZZY" THURSTON

BUFORD "BABY" RAY

GILBERT "GRAVEDIGGER" BROWN

FRANK "FRANKIE BAGGADONUTS" WINTERS

MARK "CHEWY" OHMURA

DON "MAJIK MAN" MAJKOWSKI

CHESTER "THE POLISH PRINCE" MARCOL

LARRY "THE ROCK" MCCARREN

JOHNNY "BLOOD" MCNALLY

ROBERT "CAL" HUBBARD

AUGUST "MIKE" MICHALSKE

TONY "THE GRAY GHOST OF GONZAGA" CANADEO

TRAVIS "THE ROADRUNNER" WILLIAMS

SPECIAL

111 DAVANTE ADAMS, WR

Adams caught **111** passes in 2018, coming within one catch of tying Sterling Sharpe's record for most pass receptions by a Packer in a single season. Held out of the season finale against the Lions, Adams surely would have broken Sharpe's record had he played against Detroit. He tallied 1,386 yards and scored 13 touchdowns on the year.

10 IRV COMP, DB, RB

Comp intercepted a whopping **10** passes in 1943, which remains a Packers' single season record. What's more, Comp accomplished this feat in only 10 games – which means he basically intercepted one pass every game for the entire season! The passing game wasn't a big deal then either.

1,883 AHMAN GREEN, RB

Green absolutely annihilated Jim Taylor's single-season rushing mark by more than 400 yards in leading Green Bay's potent ground attack in 2003. The **1,883**-yard season is as close as any Packer rusher has ever come to the exclusive, 2,000-yard club.

176 PAUL HORNUNG, RB

Although his record has since been broken by the Chargers' LaDainian Tomlinson, Hornung's **176** points in 1960 remains one of not only the Packers, but the NFL's greatest achievements. The 176 points came on 15 TDs, the same number of field goals, and 41 extra points. And, all the more remarkable, this was in a 12-game season!

SEASONS

17   DON HUTSON, WR

Like a number of Packers greats, it was not easy to single out a single season, but in the case of Don Hutson, 17 was the number that stood out most to me. His **17**-touchdown season in 1942 was a LEAGUE record for pass reception TDs until broken by Mark Clayton in '84. Hutson's 17 TDs topped Packers' passing records for more than fifty years, until broken by Sterling Sharpe in 1994.

4,643   AARON RODGERS, QB

Like Hutson, A-Rod has rewritten the Packers' record book to the extent that naming one single-season statistic proved difficult! Consider: A-Rod threw 45 touchdown passes in 2011 (an MVP season), and that same year, he threw for **4,643** yards, breaking Lynn Dickey's team record. Since Dickey's mark stood for nearly thirty years, I'm going with this stat – although, as I say, tough to pick just one!

112   STERLING SHARPE, WR

One-hundred-catch seasons might be commonplace in today's pass-happy NFL, but attaining the century mark for catches was a rarity when Sharpe set this **112**-reception mark in 1993. It broke his own record of 108 pass receptions set just one year prior to that!

19   JIM TAYLOR, RB

The bruising fullback was league MVP in 1962, with an amazing **19** scores on a league-leading (and longtime Packers record) 1,474 yards. It was the only year between '57 and '65 that Browns legend Jim Brown didn't lead the league in rushing! Taylor's 19 TDs was another longstanding Packers mark until broken by Ahman Green's amazing 20 touchdowns in 2003.

SPECIAL SEASONS
CONTINUED

16

REGGIE WHITE, DE

Even at the tail-end of his career, the Minister of Defense still amassed **16** sacks in 1998, which resulted in him being named NFL Defensive Player of the Year. He recorded 68.5 sacks during his six years as a Packer, and 198 for his career, good for second place all time.

*9

CHARLES WOODSON, CB

Charles "don't call me Chuck" Woodson was named Defensive Player of the Year in 2009. His stats included a career-high **nine** interceptions, which included three pick-sixes. The freewheeling Woodson, who was used all over the field, also recorded 74 tackles and two sacks. (*Eight other Packers have intercepted nine passes in a single season.)

HONORABLE MENTION:

39

BRETT FAVRE, QB

In the second of his three MVP seasons, the Gunslinger pitched **39** touchdown passes in '96, which remained a Packers record for 15 years.

1,519

JORDY NELSON, WR

1,519 was the number of receiving yards Jordy amassed in 2014- setting a team record in the process. He also had 98 receptions.

Paul Hornung's 176 points in 1960 occurred in a twelve-game season, meaning this record has never officially been broken.

GREAT

*4 WILLIE BUCHANON, CB

Two picks in a game would likely net a defensive back Defensive Player of the Week honors. But **four**? Willie achieved this feat in a game at San Diego in 1978. Ironically, he would later play for the Chargers. (*Bobby Dillon also picked off four passes in a 1953 contest at Detroit.)

299 LYNN DICKEY, QB

How do you throw for **299** yards in a snowstorm? Dickey did just that in the famous "Snow Bowl" 21-0 win over Tampa Bay in 1985. He did not throw a TD pass, but that was the only caveat to an otherwise tremendous offensive showing played in miserable weather.

154.9 BRETT FAVRE, QB

Out of all of his great games, his unbelievable 399-yard, 4 TD, **154.9** passer rating stats against Oakland in 2003 is undoubtedly one of his best. It was certainly the most memorable, coming shortly after the death of his dad, Irvin. The Pack led 31-7 at halftime.

*480 MATT FLYNN, QB

The Packers backup parlayed this monster, **480**-yard, 6-TD game against the Lions in the 2012 regular season finale into a big free agent contract with Seattle. However, that deal never panned out for him as a certain QB named "Russell Wilson" came onto the scene. (*Aaron Rodgers would equal, but not surpass, this single-season yardage mark one year later.)

GAMES

BY THE NUMBERS

218 AHMAN GREEN, RB

Like Favre, Rodgers, and Hutson, Green's name comes up repeatedly in Packer record books. In a December '03 home contest against Denver, he ran for **218** yards, shattering his own single-game Packers mark, set earlier that year.

5 VONNIE HOLLIDAY, DE

A number-one draft pick in 1998, Holliday registered not two, or even three, but **FIVE** sacks in a 2002 game against the Buffalo Bills. In addition to setting Bills QB Drew Bledsoe on his rear a handful of times, Holliday also forced three fumbles in the contest.

5 PAUL HORNUNG, RB

Five was also a big number for the once-Golden Boy of Green Bay. The star halfback was a shell of his former self, but Hornung, always a money player, came up big in 1965 when he scored five touchdowns in a road contest against Baltimore. Later that same season, Hornung rushed for 105 yards and a touchdown as Green Bay beat Cleveland for the '65 championship.

257 BILLY HOWTON, WR

This was the number of receiving yards Howton recorded in a 1956 contest against the Rams. Even more unreal, Howton amassed this total on just seven receptions, which breaks out into more than 36 yards for each catch! (Not even the great Don Hutson holds this Packers record.)

29 DON HUTSON, WR

In perhaps the best quarter of football anyone ever played, and in his last season no less, Hutson tallied **29** points on four touchdowns (and kicked five PATs) in the second quarter in a 1945 contest against the Lions. (As a team, the Packers scored six TDs against the hapless Lions in the quarter, which accounts for Hutson's additional PAT.) Think of it: 29 points, including four touchdowns, in not just a game or half, but a single quarter. Let that sink in. It's a league mark that remains to this day.

*6 AARON RODGERS, QB

Rodgers's name is littered all over the Packers' record books, and so it isn't easy to zero in on a number as his greatest performance! Let's go with this one: The future Hall of Famer tossed **six** touchdowns in a 2012 game against the Houston Texans. (Technically, this one goes down as a pair of greatest games, as A-Rod also hurled six TDs against the Bears in 2014. *Matt Flynn also tossed six touchdowns in 2012 versus the Lions.)

HONORABLE MENTION:
410 DON HORN, QB

The 1967 number-one draft pick out of San Diego State was supposed to be Bart Starr's heir apparent, but it never quite turned out that way. Still, Horn threw for five TDs and **410** yards in a 1969 contest against the St. Louis Cardinals. The yardage stood as a Packers' record for 11 years until broken by Lynn Dickey in 1980.

BEAR

Since the oldest rivalry in the NFL will take center stage in the 2019 NFL season opener at Soldier Field in the Windy City, it seemed a good time to highlight Packers who have had big games against the Chicago Bears over the years – what I call "Bear Slayers."

176   AHMAN GREEN, RB

The Packers standout rusher ran for **176** yards on only 19 carries in a 38-23 win over the Bears in Chicago in 2003.

151.2   AARON RODGERS, QB

Rodgers amassed a near-perfect **151.2** quarterback rating in a 38-17 September 2014 victory at Chicago.

99   BRETT FAVRE, ROBERT BROOKS

The QB-WR combo hooked up on a **99**-yard touchdown in a Packers' 27-24 win on Monday Night in the Windy City in September 1995. Brooks caught the ball at the Green Bay 32 and ran the remaining 68 yards untouched for a TD that put the Packers up 21–0 in the second quarter.

SLAYERS

BY THE NUMBERS

95 STEVE ODOM, KR, WR

Steve Odom, a standout kick returner, grabbed a punt and dashed **95** yards in a Packers' 20-3 victory over Chicago in 1974. It remains the longest punt return in Packers history.

75 AARON RODGERS, RANDALL COBB

Packers fans have numerous memories of Cobb, now a Dallas Cowboy, and none was sweeter than his **75**-yard TD that beat the Bears 24-23 in September 2018. (Unfortunately, it was one of few bright spots in a 6-9-1 season. But at least they beat the Bears.)

48 AARON RODGERS, RANDALL COBB

While not as long as his 75-yard Bear beater, this TD was even more memorable, as the Rodgers-Cobb **48**-yard hookup beat the Bears in thrilling fashion; 33-28 to win the NFC North in December 2013. Like Rodgers, Cobb was a big Bear Slayer during his Packers career.

39 AARON RODGERS, QB

Rodgers completed **39** passes in 56 attempts, including three touchdowns, in a 26-10 Packers win at Lambeau Field in October 2016. The Bears fell to 1-6 with the loss.

6 AARON RODGERS, QB

Rodgers threw 6 TD passes to tie the Packers team record, and match the NFL record for a half, as the Packers routed the Bears 55-14 on a Sunday night in Green Bay in November 2014.

5 BRETT FAVRE, QB

On a heavily-taped, swollen ankle, Favre incredibly still threw for 5 touchdowns in a Packers 35-28 win over the Bears in Green Bay in 1995. It was the first of his three-straight MVP seasons.

4 JIM TAYLOR, RB

Taylor rushed for 4 touchdowns as the Packers routed the Bears 38-7 in a November 1962 game in Chicago.

UNSUNG HEROES

DON BEEBE, WR
1996

Decimated by injuries at the wide receiver position, the Packers needed someone to step up, and Beebe, the former Buffalo Bill, was up to the task --- particularly when the speedy veteran caught 11 passes for 220 yards in an overtime win over San Francisco. Only two Packers receivers: Billy Howton (257 vs. the Rams in 1956) and Don Hutson (237 against Brooklyn in 1943) ever had better receiving days for the Pack. By the way: The swift Beebe also returned a kickoff for a touchdown in a regular season win at Chicago.

ZEKE BRATKOWSKI, QB*
1965

Under "Uncle Zekie", an ideal backup quarterback to Bart Starr, the Packers' offense seldom skipped a beat if Bart got hurt. Never was he better than in a Western Conference playoff game against the Baltimore Colts in 1965. Relieving the injured Starr early in the game, Bratkowski guided the Packers to a 13-10 overtime win at Lambeau Field.

KEN ELLIS, DB*
1972

Winning seasons were few and very far between after Vince Lombardi left, but one of them was in 1972, when the surprising, Dan Devine-led Packers went 10-4 and won the NFC Central Division. Bulldozing running back John Brockington, and standout rookie kicker Chester Marcol were two of the biggest reasons, but Ellis's contributions were key as well. The first-team All-Pro recovered two fumbles and intercepted four passes, including a pick-six in a 34-24 win over the 49ers. As if that wasn't enough, in the largely pre-specialist era, Ellis was also a solid punt and kickoff returner – including an 80-yard punt return in a victory over the Lions.

BEEBE, DON

BRATKOWSKI, ZEKE

ELLIS, KEN

DOUG EVANS, CB
1996

Everyone remembers the Packers beat the Patriots 35-21 in Super Bowl XXXI, but few likely recall the role Evans played in them getting there. Suffering injury upon injury, the Packers were reeling with back-to-back midseason losses to Kansas City and Dallas. The 8-3 Packers were on their way to yet another loss at the hands of the lowly Rams, when an Evans' pick-six woke the team out of their funk. They did not lose another game that season.

MATT FLYNN, QB
2013

When Aaron Rodgers was hurt early in the season with a broken collarbone against the Bears in '13, the Packers' level of quarterback play went down drastically. Journeyman veteran Seneca Wallace was not up to the task, and the younger, strong-armed Scott Tolzien was little better. What now? Thompson brought Flynn back for his second tour of duty as Packers' backup to Rodgers. Flynn was not great, but he was good enough to keep the Packers in the hunt until Rodgers returned in time to gun down the Bears in the regular season finale to win the NFC North.

CHUCK MERCEIN, RB
1967

Most Packers fans are aware that their beloved team won the Ice Bowl on a 1-yard sneak by Bart Starr. But mention the name "Chuck Mercein" and you would likely draw a few stares. Green Bay's vaunted rushing game was a mere shell of its former self (with Hornung and Taylor) and reinforcements were needed. Lombardi summoned Mercein, released from the Giants, to help fill the void. Mercein played a key role in the Packers' winning touchdown drive. But the famous photo in which he was supposedly holding up his arms to signal Starr's touchdown? Not really. Mercein actually threw his arms in the air to be sure he wouldn't be penalized for helping push Starr in for the score.

EVANS, DOUG

FLYNN, MATT

MERCEIN, CHUCK

Heritage Auction Collection

Creative Commons, Gabriel Cervantes

Mark Forsch Collection

B.J. RAJI, DT
2010

It's one thing to be a stalwart defensive tackle, plugging the middle as a DT is supposed to. As the Packers' #1 draft pick in 2009, Raji filled the bill there. But dropping into coverage to record a pick-six against the Bears in the 2010 NFC Championship Game? Unlikely. VERY unlikely in fact. A play that will always live in Packers' lore.

BRUCE WILKERSON, OT
1996

Okay, maybe three players from the Packers' Super Bowl XXXI team is a bit much, but one can't overlook the contribution of this key offensive lineman. Former standout tackle Ken Ruettgers was nearing the end of the line, but the heir apparent at the position, first-round draft pick John Michels was not up to the task. Neither was Gary Brown. What to do? Wilkerson stepped in, and the Packers' vaunted offense remained on track en route to a Super Bowl title.

TRAMON WILLIAMS, CB
2010

Interceptions were a big part of the Packers' last championship run, and T. Williams was a key reason why. His game-ending pick off of Eagles QB Michael Vick sealed the Packers' playoff opener against Philly. The next week, he did even better than that. His first interception off Matt Ryan thwarted an Atlanta drive, and his pick-six toward the end of the first half, really swung the momentum in the Packers' favor, as they coasted to victory over the top-seeded Falcons.

RAJI, B.J.

WILKERSON, BRUCE

WILLIAMS, TRAMON

WILLIE WOOD, S'
1967

Any devout Packers fan knows that Green Bay beat the Kansas City Chiefs handily in the first Super Bowl, 35-10. But many fans likely don't realize that the score was a surprisingly close 14-10 Packers lead at intermission. Chiefs QB Len Dawson had the Chiefs on the move early in the second half, but Wood picked off an errant Dawson throw and returned it 50 yards. The Packers quickly scored and never looked back.

Mark Forsech Collection

WOOD, WILLIE

SPECIAL TEAMERS

AL CARMICHAEL, RB*
1953-58

Carmichael was a solid player on some lousy Packers teams. He ranks second in most career kickoff return yards (behind Steve Odom). He raced 106 yards for a touchdown versus the Chicago Bears in 1956, a record that stood for 55 years until broken by Randall Cobb in 2011.

DON CHANDLER, K*
1965-67

The Packers were in dire need of a kicker when Vince Lombardi acquired him from the Giants. He would later boot four field goals against Oakland in Super Bowl II, but first he bombed a 90-yard punt against the 49ers in '65. His two FGs also beat the Colts in a '65 playoff game – although the Colts insist to this day that the FG that tied the game at 10 (forcing an OT) sailed wide of the uprights.

DAVE HAMPTON, RB
1969-71

Hampton only played for the Packers for three seasons, but he made a lasting mark on special teams. He ranks second in Packers annals in kickoff return yards in a season, and fourth all time in kick returns, including a 101-yarder against the Vikings in 1970.

CARMICHAEL, AL

CHANDLER, DON

HAMPTON, DAVE

CRAIG HENTRICH, P
1993-97

Hentrich ranks highly in team punting annals, and went on to even greater success with Tennessee, making the Pro Bowl twice with the Titans. Packers GM Ron Wolf once said that letting Hentrich leave in free agency was a mistake.

DESMOND HOWARD, WR
1996, 99

Howard dashed 99 yards on a kickoff return against New England in Super Bowl XXXI, and he remains the only special teams player to be named Super Bowl MVP. Howard returned three punts for touchdowns in the regular season, and one against the 49ers in a divisional playoff game. He holds team records for most punt return yardage in a single game and season.

MICAH HYDE, CB, S
2013-16

Hyde was a solid reserve and spot starter during his time in GB, but he really made his mark on special teams, where he returned three punt returns for touchdowns, including a 93-yarder against Minnesota in 2013.

HENTRICH, CRAIG

HOWARD, DESMOND

HYDE, MICAH

TIM MASTHAY, P
2010-15

Masthay, sometimes referred to as the "Red Wolverine" due to his red hair and love of the Marvel X-Men movies, is an overlooked special teams standout in Packer annals. He ranks first in highest gross average for both a single season (2011) and career.

STEVE ODOM, WR
1974-79

The small, but shifty Odom still holds the team record for longest punt return (95 yards vs. Bears in 74). He fares even better in kickoff returns in Packer annals, where he ranks first in career kickoff return yardage.

ROELL PRESTON, WR
1997-98

Preston only played for the Packers for two years, but what an impact he made as a kickoff returner! Preston ranks first in career yardage in team annals, and first in kickoff return yards in a single game. He brought two of those boots back for touchdowns.

MASTHAY, TIM

Creative Commons, Gabriel Cervantes

ODOM, STEVE

Card and Coin/Packer City Antiques

PRESTON, ROELL

Card and Coin/Packer City Antiques

TRAVIS WILLIAMS, RB[*]
1967-70

The "Roadrunner" burst on the scene as a rookie in '67, returning an unbelievable four – count 'em FOUR – touchdowns that year, including two in a single game (against the Browns). But the Roadrunner was never able to recreate his first-year magic, and was traded to the Rams. He died of heart failure in 1991 at age 45.

Travis Williams's record of four kickoff returns for touchdowns in a single season (1967) surpassed even Desmond Howard's total of three punt returns for TDs in a regular season (1996).

WILLIAMS, TRAVIS

Mark Forseth Collection

PACKERS TRIVIA

1A. Before the NFL Draft existed, college players could sign with any team they wanted. A certain future Packers star had signed a contract with two teams. The Packers had an earlier signing date, and so it was declared this player should go to Green Bay. Which player did the Packers nearly lose to another team?

1B. Bonus, which team did this future GB star nearly play for?

2. What Packers defensive lineman was nicknamed "Hawg"?

3. What Packers defensive lineman later wrestled professionally? What was his wrestling name?

4. What Packers player hails from Chico, California?

5. What Packers quarterback later appeared as Capt. Bubba Skinner on the TV series In the Heat of the Night? What was the name he used as an actor?

6. What Packers defensive great played "Bogdanski" in the 1974 movie The Longest Yard?

7. What Oakland Raiders defensive star played one year for the Packers?

8. What Packers player was nicknamed "Quickie" when he was a kid?

9. What Packers running back of the early 2000s was from Nigeria?

10. George Greene played defensive back for the Packers from 1986-1990 – but he was much better known by his nickname. What was it?

11. Charles Goldenberg was better known by what nickname?

12. What Packers offensive lineman of the '60s was better known by his nickname, "Fuzzy"?

13. What Packers receiver of the '60s and early '70s had a high school football stadium named in his honor?

14. What Dallas Cowboys defensive lineman did Packers guard Jerry Kramer block successfully to spring Bart Starr's game-winning quarterback sneak in the famous Ice Bowl?

15. What was Buford Ray's nickname?

16. What Packers great is credited with inventing the Lambeau Leap?

17. What Packers defensive tackle is credited with creating the now-famous "Summerfest" music extravaganza in Milwaukee?

18. Who was the "Minister of Defense"?

19. What 1960s Packers running back played his college ball at Philander Smith?

20. What Packers offensive lineman from 2006-2010 grew up in North Pole, Alaska?

ANSWERS

1a. Don Hutson.
1b. Brooklyn Dodgers.
2. Dave Hanner.
3. Dick Afflis, Dick the Bruiser.
4. Aaron Rodgers.
5. Carlos Brown – known in acting circles as Alan Autry.
6. Ray Nitschke.
7. Ben Davidson or Ted Hendricks.
8. Donald Driver.
9. Sambon Gado.
10. Tiger Greene.
11. "Buckets".

12. Fred Thurston.
13. Carroll Dale.
14. Jethro Pugh.
15. "Baby."
16. LeRoy Butler.
17. Henry Jordan.
18. Reggie White.
19. Elijah Pitts. It was such a small school that the joke was, "Is it Elijah Pitts from Philander Smith?" or "Philander Smith from Elijah Pitts?"
20. Daryn Colledge.

PACKER PLAYERS A-Z

A LIST OF EVERY PLAYER THAT EVER WORE THE GREEN & GOLD

PLAYER	POSITION	PACKER SEASONS	PLAYER	POSITION	PACKER SEASONS
Abbrederis, Jared	WR	2015-2016	Allen, Kenderick	DT	2006
Aberson, Cliff	RB/DB	1946	Allerman, Kurt	LB	1980-1981
Abrams, Nate	OE	1921	Allison, Geronimo	WR	2016-2018
Abramson, George	OG/OT	1925	Amsler, Marty	DE	1970
Acks, Ron	LB	1974-1976	Amundsen, Norm	OG	1957
Adams, Chet	OT/DT	1943	Anderson, Aric	LB	1987
Adams, Davante	WR	2014-2018	Anderson, Bill	OE/TE	1965-1966
Adams, Montravius	DT	2017-2018	Anderson, Donny	RB	1966-1971
Adderley, Herb	DB	1961-1969	Anderson, John	LB	1978-1989
Adkins, Bob	BB/DE	1940-1941,45	Anderson, Marques	DB	2002-2003
Affholter, Erik	WR	1991	Anderson, Vickey Ray	RB	1980
Afflis, Dick	OT/DG	1951-1954	Andruzzi, Joe	OG	1998-1999
Agajanian, Ben	K	1961	Ane, Charlie	C	1981
Aguiar, Louie	P	1999	Apsit, Marger	BB/LB	1932
Aiyewa, Victor	LB	2013	Archambeau, Lester	DE	1990-1992
Akins, Chris	DB	2000-2001	Ard, Billy	OG	1989-1991
Alcorn, Zac	TE	2006	Ariey, Mike	OT	1989
Aldridge, Bennie	DB/RB	1953	Arnold, Jahine	WR	1999
Aldridge, Lionel	DE	1963-1971	Arthur, Mike	C	1995-1996
Alexander, Jaire	DB	2018	Artmore, Rodney	DB	1999
Allen, Jake	WR	2009	Ashmore, Roger	OT	1928-1929
			Askson, Bert	TE	1975-1977
			Atkins, Steve	RB	1979-1981
			Auer, Todd	LB	1987
			Austin, Hise	DB/WR	1973
			Avery, Steve	RB	1991
			Aydelette, Buddy		1980
			Backman, Kennard	TE	2015
			Bailey, Byron	RB	1953
			Bailey, Karsten	WR	2002-2003
			Bain, Bill	OG	1975
			Baker, Bullet	RB/BB	1928-1929
			Baker, Frank	OE	1931
			Bakhtiari, David	OT	2013-2018

Mark Forsuch Collection

ALDRIDGE, LIONEL

Mark Forsch Collection

ANDERSON, BILL

PLAYER	POSITION	PACKER SEASONS	PLAYER	POSITION	PACKER SEASONS
Boedeker, Bill	RB/DB	1950	Bradford, Carl	LB	2014,16
Boerio, Chuck	LB	1952	Bradford, Corey	WR	1998-2001
Bolden, Juran	DB	1998	Bradley, Dave	OG	1969-1971
Bolston, Conrad	DT	2007	Bradley, Hunter	LS	2018
Bolton, Scott	WR	1988	Brady, Jeff	LB	1992
Bone, Warren	DE	1987	Braggs, Byron	DE	1981-1983
Bono, Steve	QB	1997	Branstetter, Kent	OT	1973
Booker, Vaughn	DE	1998-1999	Bratkowski, Zeke	QB	1963-1968, 71
Bookout, Billy	DB	1955-1956	Bray, Ray	OG/DG	1952
Boone, J.R.	RB/OE	1953	Breeland, Bashaud	DB	2018
Borak, Fred	DE	1938	Breen, Gene	LB	1964
Borden, Nate	DE	1955-1959	Brennan, Jack	OG	1939
Borgognone, Dirk	K	1995	Brice, Kentrell	DB	2016-2018
Bostick, Brandon	TE	2013-2014	Briggs, Diyral	LB	2010
Bouman, Todd	QB	2006	Brock, Charlie	C/RB	1939-1947
Bowdoin, Jim	OG	1928-1931	Brock, Lou	RB/DB	1940-1945
Bowen, Matt	DB	2001-2002	Brock, Matt	DT	1989-1994
Bowens, David	DE	2000	Brockington, John	RB	1971-1977
Bowman, Ken	C	1964-1973	Brohm, Brian	QB	2008
Boyarsky, Jerry	DT	1986-1989	Brooks, Ahmad	LB	2017
Boyd, Elmo	WR	1978	Brooks, Barrett	OT	2002
Boyd, Greg	DE	1983	Brooks, Bucky	DB	1996-1997
Boyd, Josh	DE	2013-2015	Brooks, Robert	WR	1992-1998
Boykin, Jarrett	WR	2012-2014	Bross, Mal	RB/BB	1927
Boyle, Tim	QB	2018	Broussard, Steve	P	1975
Bracken, Don	P	1985-1990	Brown, Aaron	DE	1973-1974
Brackins, Charlie	QB	1955	Brown, Allen	TE	1966-1967
			Brown, Carlos	QB	1975-1976
			Brown, Dave	DB	1987-1989
			Brown, Donatello	DB	2017
			Brown, Fadol	DE	2018
			Brown, Gary	OT	1994-1996
			Brown, Gilbert	DT	1993-1999,01-2003
			Brown, Jonathan	DE	1998
			Brown, Ken	C	1980
			Brown, Robert	DE	1982-1992
			Brown, Robert	DT	1966-1973
			Brown, Timmy	RB	1959
			Brown, Tom	DB	1964-1968
			Brown, Tony	DB	2018
			Browner, Ross	DE	1987

Card and Coin/Packer City Antiques

BISHOP, DESMOND

PLAYER	POSITION	PACKER SEASONS	PLAYER	POSITION	PACKER SEASONS
Bruder, Hank	RB/BB	1931-1939	Carlson, Wes	OG/OT	1926
Brunell, Mark	QB	1994	Carmichael, Al	RB	1953-1958
Bucchianeri, Amadeo	OG	1941,44-1945	Carpenter, Lew	RB/WR	1959-1963
Buchanon, Willie	DB	1972-1978	Carr, Fred	LB	1968-1977
Buck, Howard	OT	1921-1925	Carreker, Alphonso	DE	1984-1988
Buckley, Terrell	DB	1992-1994	Carroll, Ahmad	DB	2004-2006
Buhler, Larry	RB/BB	1939-1941	Carroll, Leo	DE	1968
Bulaga, Bryan	OT	2010-2018	Carruth, Paul Ott	RB	1986-1988
Buland, Walt	OT/OG	1924	Carson, Tra	RB	2018
Bullough, Hank	OG/LB	1955,58	Carter, Carl	DB	1992
Bultman, Art	C/LB	1932-1934	Carter, Jim	LB	1970-1975,77-1978
Burgess, Ronnie	DB	1985	Carter, Joe	OE	1942
Burks, Oren	LB	2018	Carter, Mike	WR	1970
Burnett, Morgan	DB	2010-2017	Carter, Tony	RB	2002
Burnette, Reggie	LB	1991	Casper, Cy	RB/DB	1934
Burris, Buddy	OG/LB	1949-1951	Cassidy, Ron	WR	1979-1981,83-1984
Burrow, Curtis	K	1988	Cecil, Chuck	DB	1988-1992
Burrow, Jim	DB	1976	Chandler, Don	K/RB	1965-1967
Bush, Blair	C	1989-1991	Chatman, Antonio	WR	2003-2005
Bush, Jarrett	DB	2006-2014	Cheek, Louis	OT	1991
Butler, Bill	DB/RB	1959	Cherry, Bill	C	1986-1987
Butler, Frank	C/LB	1934-1936,38	Chesley, Frank	LB	1978
Butler, LeRoy	DB	1990-2001	Childs, Henry	TE	1984
Butler, Mike	DE	1977-1982,85	Chillar, Brandon	LB	2008-2010
Byrd, Emanuel	TE	2017	Chmura, Mark	TE	1992-1999
			Choate, Putt	LB	1987
Cabral, Brian	LB	1980	Christman, Paul	QB	1950
Cade, Mossy	DB	1985-1986			
Caffey, Lee Roy	LB	1964-1969			
Cahoon, Tiny	OT	1926-1929			
Caldwell, David	DT	1987			
Callahan, Joe	QB	2016-2017			
Campbell, Ibraheim	DB	2018			
Campbell, Rich	QB	1981-1984			
Campen, James	C	1989-1993			
Canadeo, Tony	RB/DB	1941-1944,46-1952			
Cannava, Tony	RB/DB	1950			
Cannon, Mark	C	1984-1989			
Capp, Dick	TE	1967			
Capuzzi, Jim	DB/QB	1955-1956			
Carey, Joe	OG/OT	1921			

Mark Forsch Collection

BOWMAN, KEN

Player	Position	Packer Seasons
Cifelli, Gus	OT	1953
Cifers, Bob	RB	1949
Clancy, Jack	WR	1970
Clanton, Chuck	DB	1985
Claridge, Dennis	QB	1965
Clark, Allan	RB	1982
Clark, Greg	LB	1991
Clark, Jessie	RB	1983-1987
Clark, Kenny	DT	2016-2018
Clark, Michael	WR	2017
Clark, Vinnie	DB	1991-1992
Clavelle, Shannon	DE	1995-1997
Clayton, Mark	WR	1993
Clemens, Bob	RB	1955
Clemens, Cal	BB/DB	1936
Clemons, Ray	OG	1947
Clifton, Chad	OT	2000-2011
Clinton-Dix, Ha Ha	DB	2014-2018
Cloud, Jack	LB/RB	1950-1951
Cobb, Randall	WR	2011-2018
Cobb, Reggie	RB	1994
Cody, Ed	RB	1947-1948
Coffey, Junior	RB	1965
Coffman, Paul	TE	1978-1985
Cole, Colin	DT	2004-2008
Coleman, Keo	LB	1993
Colledge, Darryn	OT	2006-2010

Player	Position	Packer Seasons
Collier, Steve	OT	1987
Collins, Bobby	TE	2001
Collins, Brett	LB	1992-1993
Collins, Mark	DB	1997
Collins, Nick	DB	2005-2011
Collins, Patrick	RB	1988
Collins, Rip	RB	1951
Collins, Shawn	WR	1993
Combs, Derek	DB	2003
Comp, Irv	RB/DB	1943-1949
Compton, Chuck	DB	1987
Comstock, Rudy	OG/OT	1931-1933
Concannon, Jack	QB	1974
Cone, Fred	RB/K	1951-1957
Conway, Dave	K	1971
Cook, James	OG	1921
Cook, Jared	TE	2016
Cook, Kelly	RB	1987
Cook, Ted	OE/DB	1948-1950
Cooke, Bill	DT	1975
Cooks, Kerry	DB	1998
Cooney, Mark	LB	1974
Copeland, Russell	WR	1998
Corker, John	LB	1988
Coston, Junius	C	2005-2007
Coughlin, Frank	OT	1921
Coutre, Larry	RB	1950,53
Cox, Ron	LB	1996
Crabtree, Tom	TE	2010-2012
Craig, Larry	OE/BB	1939-1949
Crawford, James	DE	2018
Crawford, Keith	DB	1995,99
Cremer, Ted	OE/DE	1948
Crenshaw, Leon	DT	1968
Crimmins, Bernie	RB/OG	1945
Crockett, John	RB	2015
Croft, Tiny	OT	1942-1947
Cronin, Tommy	RB	1922
Crosby, Mason	K	2007-2018
Croston, Dave	OT	1988
Crouse, Ray	RB	1984

Card and Coin/Packer City Antiques

FRANKS, BUBBA

PLAYER	POSITION	PACKER SEASONS
Crowley, Jim	RB	1925
Crutcher, Tommy	LB	1964-1967,71-1972
Cuff, Ward	RB/QB	1947
Culbreath, Jim	RB	1977-1979
Culver, Al	OT	1932
Culver, Tyrone	DB	2006
Cumby, George	LB	1980-1985
Cunningham, Sederrik	WR	2013
Curcio, Mike	LB	1983
Currie, Dan	LB	1958-1964
Curry, Bill	LB	1965-1966
Curry, Scott	OT	1999
Curtin, Brennan	OT	2003
Cvercko, Andy	OG	1960
Cyre, Hector	OT/OG	1926
D'Onofrio, Mark	LB	1992
Dahms, Tom	OT	1955
Dale, Carroll	WR	1965-1972
Danelo, Joe	K	1975
Daniel, Robertson	DB	2015
Daniell, Ave	OT	1937
Daniels, Mike	DT	2012-2018
Danjean, Ernie	LB	1957
Darkins, Chris	RB	1997
Darling, Bernie	C	1927-1931
Davenport, Najeh	RB	2002-2005
Davenport, Wayne	RB	1931
Davey, Don	DT	1991-1994
Davidson, Ben	DE	1961
Davis, Anthony	LB	1999
Davis, Dave	WR	1971-1972
Davis, Harper	DB	1951
Davis, Kenneth	RB	1986-1988
Davis, Knile	RB	2016
Davis, Pahl	OG/OE	1922
Davis, Ralph	OG	1947-1948
Davis, Robert	C	1997-2007
Davis, Trevor	WR	2016-2018
Davis, Tyrone	TE	1997-2003
Davis, Willie	DE/DT	1960-1969

PLAYER	POSITION	PACKER SEASONS
Dawson, Dale	K	1988
Dawson, Gib	RB	1953
Day, Dillon	OL	2017
Dean, Walter	RB	1991
Deeks, Don	OT/OG	1948
Dees, Bob	DT/OT	1952
Degrate, Tony	DT	1985
Del Gaizo, Jim	QB	1973
Del Greco, Al	K	1984-1987
DeLisle, Jim	DT	1971
Dellenbach, Jeff	OG	1996-1998
DeLuca, Tony	DT	1984
Dendy, Patrick	DB	2005-2006
Dennard, Preston	WR	1985
Dent, Burnell	LB	1986-1992
Deschaine, Dick	K	1955-1957
Detmer, Ty	QB	1993,95
Dial, Quinton	DE	2017
Dickey, Lynn	QB	1976-1977,79-1985
Didier, Clint	TE	1988-1989
Diggs, Na'il	LB	2000-2005
Dillon, Bobby	DB	1952-1959
Dilweg, Anthony	QB	1989-1990
Dilweg, Lavvie	OE	1927-1934
Dimler, Rich	DT	1980
Dingle, Antonio	DT	1999
DiPierro, Ray	OG	1950-1951

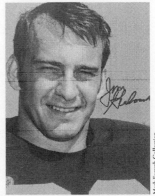

Mark Forsech Collection

GRABOWSKI, JIM

PLAYER	POSITION	PACKER SEASONS
Disend, Leo	OT	1940
Dittrich, John	OG	1959
Dominguez, Ray	OT	2011
Don Carlos, Waldo	C	1931
Donnerson, Kendall	LB	2018
Donohoe, Mike	TE	1973-1974
Dorleant, Makinton	DB	2016
Dorsett, Matthew	DB	1995
Dorsey, Dean	K	1988
Dorsey, John	LB	1984-1988
Dorsey, Kevin	WR	2013-2014
Dotson, Earl	OT	1993-2002
Dotson, Santana	DT	1996-2001
Douglass, Bobby	QB	1978
Douglass, Mike	LB	1978-1985
Dowden, Corey	DB	1996
Dowden, Steve	OT	1952
Dowler, Boyd	WR/DE	1959-1969
Dowling, Brian	QB	1977
Drechsler, Dave	OG	1983-1984
Dreyer, Wally	DB/RB	1950
Driver, Donald	WR	1999-2012
Drost, Jeff	DT	1987
Drulis, Chuck	OG/LB	1950
Duckett, Forey	DB	1994
Duford, Dukes	OE/RB	1924
Duhart, Paul	RB/DB	1944

PLAYER	POSITION	PACKER SEASONS
Dukes, Jamie	C	1994
DuMoe, Billy	OE	1921
Dunaway, Dave	WR	1968
Duncan, Ken	P	1971
Dunn, Red	BB/RB	1927-1931
Dunnigan, Pat	OT/OG	1922
Ealy, Biren	WR	2009
Earhart, Ralph	RB	1948-1949
Earp, Jug	C/OT	1922-1932
Eason, Roger	OG	1949
Ecker, Ed	DT/OT	1950-1951
Edwards, Antuan	DB	1999-2003
Edwards, Earl	DT	1979
Ellerson, Gary	RB	1985-1986
Elliott, Carl	DE/OE	1951-1954
Elliott, Jayrone	LB	2014-2016
Elliott, Tony	DE	1987
Ellis, Gerry	RB	1980-1986
Ellis, Ken	DB	1970-1975
Enderle, Dick	OG	1976
Engebretsen, Tiny	OT/OG	1934-1941
Engelmann, Wuert	RB/DB	1930-1933
Enright, Rex	RB	1926-1927
Epps, Phil	WR	1982-1988
Estep, Mike	OG	1987
Ethridge, Joe	TE/OT	1949
Evans, Dick	OE	1940,43
Evans, Doug	DB	1993-1997
Evans, Jack	BB	1929
Evans, Jahri	OG	2017
Evans, Lon	OG/OT	1933-1937
Evans, Marwin	DB	2016-2017
Fackrell, Kyler	LB	2016-2018
Falkenstein, Tony	RB/BB	1943
Fanucci, Mike	DE	1974
Faverty, Hal	LB/DE	1952
Favre, Brett	QB	1992-2007
Feasel, Greg	OT	1986
Feathers, Beattie	RB/DB	1940

Mark Forseth Collection

KOONCE, GEORGE

Mark Forseth Collection

KRAMER, JERRY

Mark Forseth Collection

HANNER, DAVE

Player	Position	Packer Seasons		Player	Position	Packer Seasons
Hansen, Don	LB	1976-1977		Hayes, Dave	OE	1921-1922
Hansen, Hal	RB/OE	1923		Hayes, Gary	DB	1984-1986
Hanson, Chris	P	1999		Hayes, Norb	OE/RB	1923
Harden, Derrick	WR	1987		Hayhoe, Bill	OT	1969-1973
Harden, Lee	DB	1970		Hays, George	DE/OE	1953
Harding, Roger	C/LB	1949		Hayward, Casey	DB	2012-2015
Hardy, Kevin	DT	1970		Hearden, Les	RB	1924
Hargrove, Jim	RB	1987		Hearden, Tom	RB	1927-1928
Harper, Chris	WR	2013		Heath, Stan	QB	1949
Harrell, Graham	QB	2010-2012		Hefner, Larry	LB	1972-1975
Harrell, Justin	DT	2007-2008,10		Heimburger, Craig	C	1999
Harrell, Willard	RB	1975-1977		Held, Paul	QB	1955
Harris, Al	DB	2003-2009		Helluin, Jerry	DT	1954-1957
Harris, Alonzo	RB	2015		Henderson, William	RB	1995-2006
Harris, Bernardo	LB	1995-2001		Hendrian, Dutch	RB/BB	1924
Harris, Corey	DB	1992-1994		Hendricks, Ted	LB	1974
Harris, DuJuan	RB	2012-2014		Henry, Urban	DT	1963
Harris, Jack	RB/OE	1925-1926		Hentrich, Craig	P	1993-1997
Harris, Jackie	TE	1990-1993		Herber, Arnie	RB/DB	1930-1940
Harris, Leotis	OG	1978-1983		Herron, Noah	RB	2005-2006
Harris, Raymont	RB	1998		Hickman, Larry	RB	1960
Harris, Tim	LB	1986-1990		Highsmith, Don	RB	1973
Harris, William	TE	1990		Hill, Don	RB/C	1929
Harrison, Anthony	DB	1987		Hill, Jim	DB	1972-1974
Hart, Derek	LS	2017		Hill, Michael	RB	2013
Hart, Doug	DB	1964-1971		Hill, Nate	DE	1988
Hartnett, Perry	OG	1987		Hilton, John	TE	1970
Hartwig, Keith	WR	1977				
Harvey, Maurice	DB	1981-1983				
Hasselbeck, Matt	QB	1999-2000				
Hathcock, Dave	DB	1966				
Hauck, Tim	DB	1991-1994				
Havig, Dennis	OG	1977				
Havner, Spencer	LB	2008-2010				
Hawk, A.J.	LB	2006-2014				
Hawkins, Josh	DB	2016-2017				
Hawkins, Michael	DB	2005				
Hawthorne, Michael	DB	2003-2004				
Haycraft, Ken	OE	1930				
Hayden, Aaron	RB	1997				
Hayes, Chris	DB	1996				

HARRIS, BERNARDO

PLAYER	POSITION	PACKER SEASONS	PLAYER	POSITION	PACKER SEASONS
Himes, Dick	OT	1968-1977	Huckleby, Harlan	RB	1980-1985
Hinkle, Clarke	RB/LB	1932-1941	Hudson, Bob	RB	1972
Hinte, Hal	OE	1942	Huffman, Tim	OG	1981-1985
Hobbins, Jim	OG	1987	Hull, Tom	LB	1975
Hodge, Abdul	LB	2006	Humphrey, Donnie	DE	1984-1986
Hoffman, Gary	OT	1984	Humphrey, Tory	TE	2005-2006,08
Holiday, Carlyle	WR	2006-2007	Hundley, Brett	QB	2015-2017
Holland, Darius	DT	1995-1997	Hunt, Cletidus	DE	1999-2004
Holland, Johnny	LB	1987-1993	Hunt, Ervin	DB	1970
Holler, Ed	LB	1963	Hunt, Kevin	OT	1972
Holliday, Vonnie	DE	1998-2002	Hunt, Mike	LB	1978-1980
Hollinquest, Lamont	LB	1996-1998	Hunter, Art	C/OT	1954
Holmberg, Rob	LB	2001	Hunter, Jason	DE	2006-2008
Holmes, Darick	RB	1998	Hunter, Scott	QB	1971-1973
Holmes, Jerry	DB	1990-1991	Hunter, Tony	RB	1987
Hood, Estus	DB	1978-1984	Hutchins, Paul	OT	1993-1994
Hope, Charles	OG	1994	Hutson, Don	OE/DB	1935-1945
Horn, Don	QB	1967-1970	Hyde, Micah	DB	2013-2016
Hornung, Paul	RB/QB	1957-1962,64-1966	Hyland, Bob	C	1967-1969,76
Horton, Jason	DB	2004-2005			
House, Davon	DB	2011-2014,17-2018	Ilkin, Tunch	OL	1993
Houston, Bobby	LB	1990	Iman, Ken	C	1960-1963
Howard, Desmond	WR	1996,99	Ingalls, Bob	C	1942
Howard, Lynn	OE/RB	1921-1922	Ingram, Darryl	TE	1992-1993
Howell, John	RB	1938	Ingram, Mark	WR	1995
Howton, Billy	OE	1952-1958	Isbell, Cecil	RB/DB	1938-1942
Hubbard, Cal	OT/OE	1929-1933,35	Ivery, Eddie Lee	RB	1979-1986
			Jacke, Chris	K	1989-1996
			Jackson, Alcender	OG	2002
			Jackson, Brandon	RB	2007-2010
			Jackson, Chris	WR	2002-2003
			Jackson, Darius	RB	2018
			Jackson, Don	RB	2016
			Jackson, Grady	DT	2003-2005
			Jackson, James	RB	2004
			Jackson, Johnnie	DB	1992
			Jackson, Joshua	DB	2018
			Jackson, Keith	TE	1995-1996
			Jackson, Melvin	OG	1976-1980
			Jacobs, Allen	RB	1965

Card and Coin/Packer City Antiques

PITTS, ELIJAH

PLAYER	POSITION	PACKER SEASONS	PLAYER	POSITION	PACKER SEASONS
Jacobs, Jack	RB/QB	1947-1949	Johnson, Sammy	RB	1979
Jacunski, Harry	OE	1939-1944	Johnson, Tom	DT	1952
Jakes, Van	DB	1989	Johnston, Swede	RB/LB	1931,34-1938
Jamerson, Natrell	DB	2018	Jolly, Johnny	DT	2006-2009,13
James, Claudis	WR	1967-1968	Jolly, Mike	DB	1980,82-1983
Janet, Ernie	OG	1975	Jones, Aaron	RB	2017-2018
Janis, Jeff	WR	2014-2017	Jones, Bob	OG	1934
Jankowski, Eddie	RB	1937-1941	Jones, Boyd	OT	1984
Jansante, Val	OE/DE	1951	Jones, Brad	LB	2009-2014
Jay, Craig	TE	1987	Jones, Bruce	OG	1927-1928
Jean-Francois, Ricky	DT	2017	Jones, Calvin	RB	1996
Jefferson, John	WR	1981-1984	Jones, Daryll	DB	1984-1985
Jefferson, Norman	DB	1987-1988	Jones, Datone	DE	2013-2016
Jenke, Noel	LB	1973-1974	Jones, Jamal	WR	2005
Jenkins, Billy	DB	2001	Jones, James	WR	2007-2013,15
Jenkins, Cullen	DT	2004-2010	Jones, Josh	DB	2017-2018
Jennings, Greg	WR	2006-2012	Jones, Ron	TE	1969
Jennings, Jim	DE/OE	1955	Jones, Scott	OT	1991
Jennings, M.D.	DB	2011-2013	Jones, Sean	DE	1994-1996
Jennison, Ray	OT	1931	Jones, Terry	DT	1978-1984
Jensen, Greg	C	1987	Jones, Tom	OG	1938
Jensen, Jim	RB	1981-1982	Jordan, Charles	WR	1994-1995,99
Jervey, Travis	RB	1995-1998	Jordan, Henry	DT/DE	1959-1969
Jeter, Bob	DB	1963-1970	Jordan, Ken	LB	1987
John, Ulrick	OT	2017	Jorgensen, Carl	OT	1934
Johnson, Bill	DE	1941	Josue, Steve	LB	2004
Johnson, Charles	DT	1979-1980,83	Joyner, Seth	LB	1997
Johnson, Chris	DB	2003			
Johnson, Danny	LB	1978			
Johnson, Ezra	DE	1977-1987			
Johnson, Glenn	OT	1949			
Johnson, Howard	OG/LB	1940-1941			
Johnson, Joe	DE	2002-2003			
Johnson, Joe	RB/OE	1954-1958			
Johnson, Kenneth	DB	1987			
Johnson, Keshon	DB	1994			
Johnson, LeShon	RB	1994-1995			
Johnson, Marvin	DB/RB	1952-1953			
Johnson, Quinn	RB	2009-2010			
Johnson, Randy	QB	1976			
Johnson, Reggie	TE	1994,97			

JONES, AARON

Card and Coin/Packer City Antiques

PLAYER	POSITION	PACKER SEASONS	PLAYER	POSITION	PACKER SEASONS
Jue, Bhawoh	DB	2001-2004	Kinard, Billy	DB/RB	1957-1958
Jurkovic, John	DT	1991-1995	Kinder, Randy	DB	1997
			King, David	DB	1987
Kahler, Bob	DB/RB	1942-1944	King, Don	DB	1987
Kahler, Royal	OT	1942	King, Don	DT/DE	1956
Kampman, Aaron	DT	2002-2009	King, Kevin	DB	2017-2018
Kapinos, Jeremy	P	2008-2009	Kirby, Jack	RB/DB	1949
Katalinas, Leo	OT/OG	1938	Kitson, Syd	OG	1980-1981,83-1984
Kauahi, Kani	C	1988	Kitts, Jim	RB	1998
Keane, Jim	OE/DE	1952	Kizer, DeShone	QB	2018
Keefe, Emmett	OG	1921	Klaus, Fee	C	1921
Kekeris, Jim	OT	1948	Klemm, Adrian	OT	2005
Kell, Paul	OT	1939-1940	Kliebhan, Adolph	RB/BB	1921
Kelley, Bill	OE	1949	Knafelc, Gary	OE	1954-1962
Kelly, Joe	LB	1995	Knapp, Lindsay	OG	1996
Kemp, Perry	WR	1988-1991	Knutson, Gene	DE	1954,56
Kendricks, Lance	TE	2017-2018	Knutson, Steve	OG	1976-1977
Kercher, Bob	OE	1944	Koart, Matt	DE	1986
Kern, Bill	OT	1929-1930	Koch, Greg	OT	1977-1985
Kerridge, Joe	RB	2016-2017	Koncar, Mark	OT	1976-1977,79-1981
Keuper, Ken	RB/DB	1945-1947	Konopasek, Ed	OT	1987
Kiel, Blair	QB	1988,90-1991	Koonce, George	LB	1992-1999
Kiesling, Walt	OG/OT	1935-1936	Kopay, Dave	RB	1972
Kight, Kelvin	WR	2004	Kostelnik, Ron	DT	1961-1968
Kilbourne, Wally	OT	1939	Kotal, Eddie	RB/BB	1925-1929
Kimball, Bobby	WR	1979-1980	Kovatch, Johnny	OE	1947
Kimmel, J.D.	DT	1958	Kowalkowski, Bob	OG	1977
			Kramer, Jerry	OG	1958-1968
			Kramer, Ron	OE/TE	1957,59-1964
			Kranz, Ken	DB	1949
			Krause, Larry	RB	1970-1971,73-1974
			Krause, Ryan	WR	2007
			Kroll, Bob	DB	1972
			Kuberski, Bob	DT	1995-1998
			Kuechenberg, Rudy	LB	1970
			Kuhn, John	RB	2007-2015
			Kumerow, Jake	WR	2018
			Kurth, Joe	OT	1933-1934
			Kuusisto, Bill	OG	1941-1946
			LaBounty, Matt	DE	1995

Mark Forseth Collection

JONES, SEAN

Card and Coin/Packer City Antiques

MANDARICH, TONY

PLAYER	POSITION	PACKER SEASONS
Luchey, Nicolas	RB	2003-2004
Lucky, Bill	DT	1955
Lueck, Bill	OG	1968-1974
Luhn, Nolan	OE	1945-1949
Luke, Steve	DB	1975-1980
Lumpkin, Kregg	RB	2008
Lusteg, Booth	K	1969
Lyle, Dewey	OG/OE	1922-1923
Lyman, Del	OT	1941
Lyon, Billy	DE	1998-2002
Maas, Bill	DT	1993
Mack, Red	WR	1966
MacLeod, Tom	LB	1973
Maddox, Buster	OT	1935
Majkowski, Don	QB	1987-1992
Malancon, Rydell	LB	1987
Malone, Alfred	DE	2008
Malone, Grover	RB/OE	1921
Mandarich, Tony	OG	1989-1991
Mandeville, Chris	DB	1987-1988
Manley, Willie	OT/OG	1950-1951
Mann, Bob	OE	1950-1954
Mann, Errol	K	1968
Manning, Brian	WR	1998
Manning, Roy	LB	2005
Manning, Terrell	LB	2012

PLAYER	POSITION	PACKER SEASONS
Mansfield, Von	DB	1987
Manuel, Marquand	DB	2006
Marcol, Chester	K	1972-1980
Marks, Larry	RB	1928
Marshall, Rich	DT	1965
Marshall, Torrance	LB	2001-2004
Martell, Herm	OE	1921
Martin, Charles	DT	1984-1987
Martin, David	TE	2001-2006
Martin, Derrick	DB	2009-2010
Martin, Ingle	QB	2006
Martin, Ruvell	WR	2006-2008
Martinez, Blake	LB	2016-2018
Martinkovic, John	DE/DT	1951-1956
Maryland, Russell	DT	2000
Mason, Dave	DB	1974
Mason, Joel	OE	1942-1945
Mason, Larry	RB	1988
Massey, Carlton	DE	1957-1958
Masters, Norm	OT	1957-1964
Masthay, Tim	P/K	2010-2015
Mataele, Stan	DT	1987
Mathys, Charlie	BB/QB	1922-1926
Matson, Pat	OG	1975
Matthews, Al	DB	1970-1975
Matthews, Aubrey	WR	1988-1989
Matthews, Clay	LB	2009-2018
Mattos, Harry	RB	1936
Matuszak, Marv	LB	1958
Mayer, Frank	OG/OT	1927
Mayes, Derrick	WR	1996-1998
Mays, Devante	RB	2017
Mays, Kivuusama	LB	1999
McAuliffe, Jack	RB	1926
McBride, Ron	RB	1973
McBride, Tod	DB	1999-2002
McCaffrey, Bob	C	1975
McCaffrey, Max	WR	2016
McCarren, Larry	C	1973-1984
McCaskill, Nevin	OT	2008
McCaslin, Eugene	LB	2000

Creative Commons, cropped

MCCOY, NIKE

PLAYER	POSITION	PACKER SEASONS	PLAYER	POSITION	PACKER SEASONS
McCloughan, Dave	DB	1992	McNally, Johnny	RB/DB	1929-1933,35-1936
McConkey, Phil	WR	1986	McPherson, Forrest	C/OG	1943-1945
McCoy, Mike	DB	1976-1983	Meade, Mike	RB	1982-1983
McCoy, Mike	DT	1970-1976	Mealey, Rondell	RB	2001-2002
McCrary, Herdis	RB/LB	1929-1933	Meilinger, Steve	OE	1958,60
McCray, Justin	OG	2017-2018	Melka, James	LB	1987
McDonald, Dustin	OG	1935	Mendoza, Ruben	OG	1986
McDonald, Nick	OG	2010	Mercein, Chuck	RB	1967-1969
McDougal, Bob	RB	1947	Mercer, Mike	K	1968-1969
McDowell, John	OT	1964	Meredith, Jamon	OT	2009
McElmurry, Blaine	DB	1997	Merling, Phillip	DE	2012
McGarrahan, Scott	DB	1998-2000	Merrill, Casey	DE	1979-1983
McGarry, John	OG	1987	Merrill, Mark	LB	1982
McGaw, Walt	OG	1926	Merriweather, Mike	LB	1993
McGeary, Clarence	DT	1950	Mestnik, Frank	RB	1963
McGee, Buford	RB	1992	Metcalf, Eric	RB	2002
McGee, Max	OE	1954,57-1967	Meyer, Jim	OT	1987
McGeorge, Rich	TE	1970-1978	Michael, Christine	RB	2016
McGill, Lenny	DB	1994-1995	Michaels, Lou	DE/K	1971
McGrew, Sylvester	DE	1987	Michaels, Walt	LB	1951
McGruder, Michael	DB	1989	Michalske, Mike	OG/OT	1929-1935,37
McGuire, Gene	C	1996	Michels, John	OT	1996-1997
McHan, Lamar	QB	1959-1960	Mickens, Terry	WR	1994-1997
McHugh, Sean	TE	2004	Middleton, Terdell	RB	1977-1981
McIlhenny, Don	RB	1957-1959	Midler, Lou	OG/OT	1940
McIntyre, Guy	OG	1994	Mihajlovich, Lou	DE	1954
McJulien, Paul	P	1991-1992	Milan, Don	QB	1975
McKay, Roy	RB/DB	1944-1947			
McKenzie, Keith	DE	1996-1999,02			
McKenzie, Mike	DB	1999-2004			
McKenzie, Raleigh	OG	1999-2000			
McLaughlin, Joe	LB	1979			
McLaughlin, Lee	OG	1941			
McLean, Ray	RB/BB	1921			
McLeod, Mike	DB	1984-1985			
McMahon, Jim	QB	1995-1996			
McMath, Herb	DT	1977			
McMichael, Steve	DT	1994			
McMillan, Ernie	OT	1975			
McMillian, Jerron	DB	2012-2013			
McNabb, Dexter	RB	1992-1993			

MICKENS, TERRY

PLAYER	POSITION	PACKER SEASONS	PLAYER	POSITION	PACKER SEASONS
Millard, Keith	DT	1992	Moore, Jason	DB	2000
Miller, Don	RB	1954	Moore, Rich	DT	1969-1970
Miller, John	LB	1987	Moore, Tom	RB	1960-1965
Miller, Johnny	OT/DT	1960	Moran, Rich	OG	1985-1993
Miller, Jordan	DT	2012	Morency, Vernand	RB	2006-2007
Miller, Ookie	C/OG	1938	Moresco, Tim	DB	1977
Miller, Paul	RB	1936-1938	Morgan, Anthony	WR	1993-1996
Miller, Tom	DE/OE	1946	Morley, Steve	OT	2004
Mills, Stan	RB/OE	1922-1923	Morris, Jim Bob	DB	1987
Minick, Paul	OG/OE	1928-1929	Morris, Larry	RB	1987
Miree, Brandon	RB	2006	Morris, Lee	WR	1987
Mitchell, Basil	RB	1999-2000	Morrison, Antonio	LB	2018
Mitchell, Charlie	DB/RB	1946	Morrissey, Jim	LB	1993
Mitchell, Roland	DB	1991-1994	Morton, Mike	LB	2000
Moffitt, Mike	TE	1986	Moselle, Dom	DB/RB	1951-1952
Moje, Dick	OE	1951	Moses, Dezman	LB	2012
Molenda, Bo	RB/BB	1928-1932	Moses, J.J.	WR	2002
Moll, Tony	OT	2006-2008	Mosley, Russ	RB	1945-1946
Monaco, Ron	LB	1987	Moss, Perry	QB	1948
Monnett, Bob	RB/DB	1933-1938	Mott, Joe	LB	1993
Monroe, Henry	DB	1979	Mott, Norm	RB/DB	1933
Montgomery, Mike	DT	2005-2010	Muir, Daniel	DT	2007
Montgomery, Ty	RB	2015-2018	Mullen, Roderick	DB	1995-1997
Moore, Allen	DE	1939	Mulleneaux, Carl	OE	1938-1941,45-1946
Moore, Blake	C	1984-1985	Mulleneaux, Lee	C/RB	1938
Moore, Brent	LB	1987	Mulumba, Andy	LB	2013-2015
Moore, J'Mon	WR	2018	Murphy, Kyle	OT	2016-2017
			Murphy, Mark	DB	1980-1985,87-1991
			Murphy, Terrence	WR	2005
			Murray, Jab	OE/OT	1921-1924

Nadolney, Peaches	OG/OT	1922
Nall, Craig	QB	2003 2005,07
Nance, Dimitri	RB	2010
Nash, Tom	OE	1928-1932
Navies, Hannibal	LB	2003-2004
Neal, Ed	OG/OT	1945-1951
Neal, Frankie	WR	1987
Neal, Mike	DT	2010-2015
Neill, Bill	DT	1984
Nelson, Bob	DT	1988-1990

Mark Forseth Collection

NEWSOME, CRAIG

Mark Forsch Collection

RISON, ANDRE

PLAYER	POSITION	PACKER SEASONS	PLAYER	POSITION	PACKER SEASONS
Pearson, Lindy	RB	1952	Ploeger, Kurt	DE	1986
Peay, Francis	OT	1968-1972	Pointer, John	LB	1987
Pederson, Doug	QB	1996-1998,01-2004	Pope, Bucky	WR	1968
Pelfrey, Ray	OE/RB	1951-1952	Pope, P.J.	RB	2006
Pennel, Mike	DT	2014-2016	Poppinga, Brady	LB	2005-2010
Pepper, Taybor	LS	2017	Porter, Joe	DB	2008
Peppers, Julius	DE	2014-2016	Powers, Sammy	OG/OT	1921
Peprah, Charlie	DB	2006-2008,10-2011	Prather, Guy	LB	1981-1985
Perillo, Justin	TE	2014-2016	Pregulman, Merv	C/OG	1946
Perkins, Don	RB	1944-1945	Prescott, Hal	OE	1946
Perko, Tom	LB	1976	Preston, Roell	WR	1997-1998
Perry, Claude	OT/OG	1927-1935	Price, Brian	DT	2016
Perry, Nick	LB	2012-2018	Prior, Mike	DB	1993-1998
Pesonen, Dick	DB	1960	Pritko, Steve	OE/DE	1949-1950
Peterson, Kenny	DE	2003-2005	Prokop, Joe	P	1985
Peterson, Les	OE/OT	1932,34	Provo, Fred	RB	1948
Peterson, Ray	RB/DB	1937	Psaltis, Jim	DB	1954
Petitbon, Johnny	DB/RB	1957	Purdy, Pid	BB	1926-1927
Pettway, Kenneth	LB	2008	Pureifory, Dave	DE	1972-1977
Petway, David	DB	1981	Purnell, Frank	RB	1957
Pickens, Bruce	DB	1993			
Pickett, Ryan	DT	2006-2013	Quarless, Andrew	TE	2010-2015
Pipkins, Lenzy	DB	2017	Quatse, Jesse	OT	1933
Pisarkiewicz, Steve	QB	1980	Query, Jeff	WR	1989-1991
Pitts, Elijah	RB	1961-1969,71	Quinlan, Bob	DE	1959-1962
Pitts, Ron	DB	1988-1990			
Pleasant, Eddie	DB	2018	Radick, Ken	OE/OG	1930-1931
			Rafferty, Vince	C	1987
			Raji, B.J.	DT	2009-2013,15
			Randall, Damarious	DB	2015-2017
			Randolph, Al	DB	1971
			Randolph, Terry	DB	1977
			Ranspot, Keith	OE	1942
			Rash, Lou	DB	1987
			Ray, Baby	OT	1938-1948
			Rayner, Dave	K	2006
			Redick, Corn	WR	1987
			Redmond, Will	DB	2018
			Regnier, Pete	RB	1922
			Reichardt, Bill	RB	1952
			Reid, Breezy	RB	1950-1956

Creative Commons

SATURDAY, JEFF

PLAYER	POSITION	PACKER SEASONS
Renner, Bill	P	1986-1987
Reynolds, Jamal	DE	2001-2003
Rhodemyre, Jay	C/LB	1948-1949,51-1952
Rice, Allen	RB	1991
Richard, Gary	DB	1988
Richardson, Sean	DB	2012-2015
Riddick, Ray	OE	1940-1942,46
Ringo, Christian	DE	2016
Ringo, Jim	C	1953-1963
Ripkowski, Aaron	RB	2015-2017
Risher, Alan	QB	1987
Rison, Andre	WR	1996
Rivera, Marco	OG	1997-2004
Roach, John	QB/DB	1961-1963
Robbins, Austin	DT	2000
Robbins, Tootie	OT	1992-1993
Roberts, Bill	RB	1956
Robinson, Bill	RB	1952
Robinson, Charley	OG/LB	1951
Robinson, Dave	LB	1963-1972
Robinson, Eugene	DB	1996-1997
Robinson, Koren	WR	2006-2007
Robinson, Luther	DE	2014
Robinson, Michael	DB	1996
Robison, Tommy	OT	1987
Roche, Alden	DE	1971-1976
Rodgers, Aaron	QB	2005-2018
Rodgers, Del	RB	1982,84
Rodgers, Richard	TE	2014-2017
Rogers, Nick	LB	2004
Rohrig, Herm	RB/DB	1941,46-1947
Rolle, Jumal	DB	2013
Roller, Dave	DT	1975-1978
Rollins, Quinten	DB	2015-2017
Roman, Mark	DB	2004-2005
Romine, Al	DB/RB	1955,58
Rosatti, Rosey	OT	1924,26-1927
Rose, Al	OE	1932-1936
Roskie, Ken	RB	1948
Ross, Dan	TE	1986
Ross, Jeremy	WR	2012-2013

PLAYER	POSITION	PACKER SEASONS
Rossum, Allen	DB	2000-2001
Rote, Tobin	QB	1950-1956
Rouse, Aaron	DB	2007-2009
Rowser, John	DB	1967-1969
Rubens, Larry	C	1982-1983
Rubley, T.J.	QB	1995
Rudzinski, Paul	LB	1978-1980
Ruegamer, Grey	C	2003-2005
Ruettgers, Ken	OT	1985-1996
Ruetz, Howie	DT	1951-1953
Rule, Gordon	DB	1968-1969
Rush, Clive	OE	1953
Ruzich, Steve	OG/LB	1952-1954
Ryan, Jake	LB	2015-2017
Ryan, Jon	P	2006-2007
Saine, Brandon	RB	2011-2012
Salem, Harvey	OT	1992
Salsbury, Jim	OG/OT	1957-1958
Sample, Chuck	RB	1942,45
Sampson, Howard	DB	1978-1979
Sams, Ron	OG	1983
Sander, B.J.	P	2005
Sandifer, Dan	DB/RB	1952-1953
Sands, Terdell	DT	2003
Sandusky, John	OT/DT	1956
Sarafiny, Al	C	1933

TAYLOR, AARON

Creative Commons, cropped

TORKELSON, ERIC

PLAYER	POSITION	PACKER SEASONS
Smith, Evan	OG/C	2009,11-2013
Smith, Jermaine	DT	1997,99
Smith, Jerry	OG/LB	1956
Smith, Kevin	RB	1996
Smith, Larry	DT	2003-2004
Smith, Maurice	RB	2002
Smith, Ollie	WR	1976-1977
Smith, Perry	DB	1973-1976
Smith, Red	RB/BB	1927,29
Smith, Rex	OE	1922
Smith, Rod	DB	1998
Smith, Warren	OG	1921
Smith, Wes	WR	1987
Smithson, Shaky	WR	2011
Snelling, Ken	RB/LB	1945
Snider, Mal	OT	1972-1974
Snider, Matt	RB	1999-2000
So'oto, Vic	LB	2011-2012
Sorenson, Glen	OG	1943-1945
Spagnola, John	TE	1989
Sparlis, Al	OG	1946
Spears, Ron	DE	1983
Spencer, Joe	OT/DT	1950-1951
Spencer, Ollie	OT/OG	1957-1958
Spilis, John	WR	1969-1971
Spinks, Jack	OG/RB	1955-1956
Spitz, Jason	OL	2006-2010
Spriggs, Jason	OT	2016-2018
Spriggs, Marcus	OT	2003
Sproul, Dennis	QB	1978
St. Brown, Equanimeous	WR	2018
Stachowicz, Ray	P	1981-1982
Staggers, Jon	WR	1972-1974
Stahlman, Dick	OT/OG	1931-1932
Stanley, Walter	WR	1985-1988
Stansauk, Don	DT/OT	1950-1951
Starch, Ken	RB	1976
Starks, James	RB	2010-2016
Staroba, Paul	WR	1973
Starr, Bart	QB	1956-1971
Starret, Ben	BB/RB	1942-1945

PLAYER	POSITION	PACKER SEASONS
Steele, Ben	TE	2004-2005
Steen, Frank	OE	1939
Steiner, Rebel	DB	1950-1951
Stenerud, Jan	K	1980-1983
Stephen, Scott	LB	1987-1991
Stephens, John	RB	1993
Stephenson, Dave	OG/C	1951-1955
Sterling, John	RB	1987
Stevens, Billy	QB	1968-1969
Stewart, Steve	LB	1979
Stills, Ken	DB	1985-1989
Stokes, Barry	OT	2000-2001
Stokes, Timothy	OT	1978-1982
Stonebraker, John	OE	1942
Stoneburner, Jake	TE	2013
Strickland, Fred	LB	1994-1995
Sturgeon, Lyle	OT	1937
Sullivan, Carl	DE	1987
Sullivan, John	DB	1986
Summerhays, Bob	LB/RB	1949-1951
Summers, Don	TE	1987
Sutton, Mickey	DB	1989
Svendsen, Earl	C/LB	1937,39
Svendsen, George	C	1935-1937,40-1941
Swain, Brett	WR	2009-2010
Swanke, Karl	OT	1980-1986
Swiney, Erwin	DB	2002-2003

Card and Coin/Packer City Antiques

WILLIAMS, TRAMON

PLAYER	POSITION	PACKER SEASONS
Switzer, Veryl	RB/DB	1954-1955
Sydney, Harry	RB	1992
Symank, John	DB	1957-1962
Szafaryn, Len	OT/OG	1950,53-1956
Tagge, Jerry	QB	1972-1974
Tassos, Damon	OG	1947-1949
Taugher, Biff	RB	1922
Tauscher, Mark	OT	2000-2010
Taylor, Aaron	OG	1994-1997
Taylor, Ben	LB	2006
Taylor, Cliff	RB	1976
Taylor, Herbert	OT	2011
Taylor, Jim	RB	1958-1966
Taylor, Kitrick	WR	1992
Taylor, Lane	OG	2013-2018
Taylor, Lenny	WR	1984
Taylor, Ryan	TE	2011-2014
Taylor, Willie	WR	1978
Teague, George	DB	1993-1995
Temp, Jim	DE	1957-1960
Tenner, Bob	OE	1935
Terrell, Pat	DB	1998
Teteak, Deral	LB/OG	1952-1956
Thibodeaux, Keith	DB	2001
Thierry, John	DE	2000-2001
Thomas, Ben	DE	1986

PLAYER	POSITION	PACKER SEASONS
Thomas, Ike	DB	1972-1973
Thomas, Joe	LB	2015-2017
Thomas, Joey	DB	2004-2005
Thomas, Lavale	RB	1987-1988
Thomas, Robert	LB	2005
Thomason, Bobby	QB	1951
Thomason, Jeff	TE	1995-1999
Thompson, Arland	OG	1981
Thompson, Aundra	WR	1977-1981
Thompson, Darrell	RB	1990-1994
Thompson, Jeremy	DE	2008-2009
Thompson, John	TE	1979-1982
Thompson, Tuffy	RB	1939
Thornburg, Jeremy	DB	2005
Thurman, Andrae	WR	2004-2005
Thurston, Fuzzy	OG	1959-1967
Timberlake, George	LB/OG	1955
Timmerman, Adam	OG	1995-1998
Tinker, Gerald	WR	1975
Tinsley, Pete	OG	1938-1945
Toburen, Nelson	LB	1961-1962
Tollefson, Charlie	OG	1944-1946
Tolzien, Scott	QB	2013-2015
Tomczak, Mike	QB	1991
Tomich, Jared	DE	2002
Toner, Tom	LB	1973,75-1977
Tonnemaker, Clay	LB/C	1950,53-1954
Tonyan, Robert	TE	2018
Toomer, Korey	LB	2018
Toribio, Anthony	DT	2008-2009
Torkelson, Eric	RB	1974-1979,81
Traylor, Keith	DT	1993
Tretter, J.C.	OT	2013-2016
Tripp, Jordan	LB	2016
Troup, Bill	QB	1980
Truluck, R-Kal	DE	2004
Tuaolo, Esera	DT	1991-1992
Tullis, Walter	WR	1978-1979
Tunnell, Emlen	DB	1959-1961
Turner, Maurice	RB	1985
Turner, Richard	DT	1981-1983

Mark Forseth Collection

WILLIAMS, TRAVIS

PLAYER	POSITION	PACKER SEASONS		PLAYER	POSITION	PACKER SEASONS
Turner, Wylie	DB	1979-1980		Wagner, Steve	DB	1976-1979
Turpin, Miles	LB	1986		Wahle, Mike	OT	1998-2004
Tuttle, George	OE	1927		Walden, Erik	DE	2010-2012
Twedell, Frank	OG	1939		Walker, Cleo	LB	1970
				Walker, Frank	DB	2007
Uecker, Keith	OT	1984-85,87-88,90-91		Walker, Javon	WR	2002-2005
Underwood, Brandon	DB	2009-2010		Walker, Josh	OG	2015
Underwood, Marviel	DB	2005		Walker, Malcolm	C	1970
Uram, Andy	RB	1938-1943		Walker, Randy	P	1974
Urban, Alex	DE/OE	1941,44-1945		Walker, Rod	DT	2001-2003
Usher, Eddie	RB	1922,24		Walker, Sammy	DB	1993
				Walker, Val Joe	DB	1953-1956
Vairo, Dom	OE	1935		Wallace, Calvin	DE	1987
Valdes-Scantling, Marquez	WR	2018		Wallace, Seneca	QB	2013
Van Dyke, Bruce	OG	1974-1976		Wallace, Taco	WR	2005
Van Every, Hal	RB/DB	1940-1941		Walls, Wesley	TE	2003
Van Roten, Greg	OG	2012-2013		Walsh, Ward	RB	1972
Van Sickle, Clyde	OG	1932-1933		Walter, Tyson	OT	2006
Van Valkenberg, Pete	RB	1974		Warren, Steve	DT	2000,02
Vandersea, Phil	LB	1966,68-1969		Washington, Chuck	DB	1987
Vanoy, Vern	DT	1972		Washington, Donnell	DT	2005
Vant Hull, Fred	OG/LB	1942		Waters, Herb	DB	2016
Vataha, Randy	WR	1977		Watts, Elbert	DB	1986
Veingrad, Alan	OT	1986-1987,89-1990		Wayne, Nate	LB	2000-2002
Verba, Ross	OG	1997-2000		Weathers, Clarence	WR	1990-1991
Vereen, Carl	OT	1957		Weatherwax, Jim	DT	1966-1967,69
Vergara, George	OE	1925		Weaver, Gary	LB	1975-1979
Viaene, David	C	1992				
Villanucci, Vince	DT	1987				
Vinson, Fred	DB	1999				
Vitale, Dan	RB	2018				
Vogds, Evan	OG	1948-1949				
Vogel, Justin	P	2017				
Voss, Lloyd	DE	1964-1965				
Voss, Tillie	OE/OT	1924				
Waddy, Jude	LB	1998-1999				
Wade, Charlie	WR	1975				
Wafer, Carl	DE	1974				
Wagner, Bryan	P	1992-1993				
Wagner, Buff	RB/BB	1921				

WILLIAMS, TYRONE

PLAYER	POSITION	PACKER SEASONS	PLAYER	POSITION	PACKER SEASONS
Webb, Chuck	RB	1991	Wicks, Bob	WR	1974
Webber, Dutch	OE/RB	1928	Widby, Ron	P	1972-1973
Webster, Tim	K	1971	Widell, Doug	OG	1993
Weddington, Mike	LB	1986-1990	Wildung, Dick	OT/DT	1946-1951,53
Wehba, Ray	OE	1944	Wilhelm, Matt	LB	2010
Weigel, Lee	RB	1987	Wilkens, Elmer	OE	1925
Weisgerber, Dick	BB/RB	1938-1940,42	Wilkerson, Bruce	OT	1996-1997
Weishuhn, Clayton	LB	1987	Wilkerson, Muhammad	DT	2018
Wellman, Mike	C	1979-1980	Wilkins, Gabe	DE	1994-1997
Wells, Don	DE/OE	1946-1949	Wilkins, Marcus	LB	2002-2003
Wells, Scott	C	2004-2011	Willhite, Kevin	RB	1987
Wells, Terry	RB	1975	Williams, A.D.	OE/WR	1959
West, Ed	TE	1984-1994	Williams, Brian	LB	1995-2000
West, Pat	RB	1948	Williams, Corey	DT	2004-2007
Westbrook, Bryant	DB	2002	Williams, D.J.	TE	2011-2012
Wetnight, Ryan	TE	2000	Williams, Delvin	RB	1981
Wheeler, Cowboy	OE	1921-1923	Williams, Gerald	DE	1997
Whitaker, Bill	DB	1981-1982	Williams, Howie	DB	1962-1963
White, Adrian	DB	1992	Williams, Jamaal	RB	2017-2018
White, Chris	OG	2005	Williams, K.D.	LB	2000-2001
White, Gene	DB	1954	Williams, Kevin	RB	1993
White, Johnny	RB	2012	Williams, Mark	LB	1994
White, Myles	WR	2013	Williams, Patrick	WR	2009
White, Reggie	DE	1993-1998	Williams, Perry	RB	1969-1973
White, Tracy	LB	2006-2008	Williams, Sweeny	DE	1970-1977
Whitehead, Jermaine	DB	2016-2018	Williams, Tramon	DB	2007-2014,18
Whitehurst, David	QB	1977-1983	Williams, Travis	RB	1967-1970
Whitley, James	DB	2003-2004	Williams, Tyrone	DB	1996-2002
Whittenton, Jesse	DB	1958-1964	Williams, Walter	RB	2004-2005
Whitticker, William	OG	2005	Willig, Matt	OT	1998

Mark Forsch Collection

Players' name, position, and years played for Packers
courtesy of The Football Database, www.footballdb.com

Mark Forseth Collection

CHAMPIONSHIP YEARS

*1929
12-0

*1930
10-3-1

*1931
12-2

* Championships were based on regular season standings, as the playoff system was not implemented until 1933.

Prominent players and their ranking in the top #100 Packers of all time:

#12 – Johnny "Blood" McNally
#14 – "Cal" Hubbard
#19 – "Mike" Michalske
#29 – Arnie Herber
#51 – Vern Lewellen
#60 – Lavvie Dilweg

1936
10-1-1

1936 NFL Championship
Green Bay 21, Boston Redskins 6

An early Arnie Herber to Don Hutson bomb started the scoring, and Green Bay never looked back.

Prominent players and their ranking in top #100 include:

#1 – Don Hutson
#10 – Clarke Hinkle
#12 – Johnny "Blood" McNally
#29 – Arnie Herber
#77 – Charles "Buckets" Goldenberg

1939
9-2

1939 NFL Championship
Green Bay 27, New York Giants 0

Milt Gantenbein caught a touchdown pass from Arnie Herber, and Joe Laws hauled in a TD pass from Cecil Isbell.

Prominent players and their top #100 ranking include:

#1 – Don Hutson
#10 – Clarke Hinkle
#29 – Arnie Herber
#42 – Cecil Isbell
#77 – Charles "Buckets" Goldenberg
#83 – Joe Laws
#94 – Buford "Baby" Ray
#97 – Charley Brock

1944
8-2

1944 NFL Championship
Green Bay 14, New York
Giants 7

Ted Fritsch scored both
Packers touchdowns in the
title game.

Prominent players and their
top #100 ranking include:

#1- Don Hutson
#8 – Tony Canadeo
#69 – Ted Fritsch
#77 – Charles "Buckets"
 Goldenberg
#83 – Joe Laws
#87 – Irv Comp
#94 – Buford "Baby" Ray
#97 – Charley Brock

1961
11-3

1961 NFL Championship
Green Bay 37, New York
Giants 0

Ron Kramer recorded a pair
of touchdowns, while Paul
Hornung and Boyd Dowler
each scored a single TD as the
Packers rolled to their first
championship since 1944 – and
over Lombardi's former team.

*Prominent players and their
top #100 ranking include:
* There are 24 Lombardi-era
Packers in the top #100 so not
all of them are listed in the
championship recaps.

#2 – Bart Starr
#5 – Forrest Gregg
#6 – Ray Nitschke
#9 – Paul Hornung
#13 – Jim Taylor
#17 – Jerry Kramer
#57 – Ron Kramer
#84 – Hank Gremminger
 (int. in '61 title game)
#85 – Fred "Fuzzy" Thurston
#91 – Jesse Whittenton
 (int. in '61 title game)

1962
13-1

1962 NFL Championship
Green Bay 16, New York
Giants 7

Jerry Kramer kicked three
field goals in cold, blustery
conditions, Jim Taylor scored a
touchdown, and Ray Nitschke
had a monster game on defense
(winning MVP honors) as the
Packers defended their title.

#5 – Forrest Gregg
#6 – Ray Nitschke
#13 – Jim Taylor
#15 – Willie Davis
#17 – Jerry Kramer
#23 – Jim Ringo
#33 – Boyd Dowler
#57 – Ron Kramer

Sources: Wikipedia, www.packershistory.net

CHAMPIONSHIP YEARS

1965
10-3-1

1965 NFL Championship
Green Bay 23, Cleveland 12

In snowy, muddy conditions, Paul Hornung and Jim Taylor ran amok through the Cleveland defense, while Green Bay's "D" held Cleveland superstar RB Jim Brown in check.

#2 – Bart Starr
#6 – Ray Nitschke
#9 – Paul Hornung
#11 – Herb Adderley
#13 – Jim Taylor
#16 – Willie Wood
#62 – Carroll Dale

1966
12-2

1966 NFL Championship
Green Bay 34, Dallas 27

In the '66 title matchup, Bart Starr threw four – yes FOUR – touchdown passes, and Dave Robinson held off a late Dallas drive that would have tied the game, by forcing Dallas QB Don Meredith into an INT.

Super Bowl I
Green Bay 35, Kansas City 10

In Super Bowl I, Max McGee famously came off the bench to catch seven passes, and Willie Wood provided a key INT, as Green Bay rolled past the AFL champions.

#2 – Bart Starr
#11 – Herb Adderley
#13 – Jim Taylor
#16 – Willie Wood
#22 – Dave Robinson
#33 – Boyd Dowler
#52 – Max McGee
#62 – Carroll Dale
#78 – Bob Jeter

1967
9-4-1

1967 NFL Championship
(Ice Bowl)
Green Bay 21, Dallas 17

The Packers were a veteran, though aging team, and trailed 17-14 late in the '67 title game, when Bart Starr led Green Bay to a winning touchdown, on his 1-yard sneak, in the famous Ice Bowl.

Super Bowl II
Green Bay 33, Oakland 14

After subzero temps in Green Bay, the Packers coasted in the sun in Super Bowl II. Key plays included a Bart Starr to Boyd Dowler score, four field goals by Don Chandler, and the first pick-six in SB history, by GB corner Herb Adderley. It was Vince Lombardi's last game as Packers coach.

#2 – Bart Starr
#6 – Ray Nitschke
#11 – Herb Adderley
#16 – Willie Wood
#17 – Jerry Kramer
#33 – Boyd Dowler
#52 – Max McGee
#62 – Carroll Dale

1996
13-3

1996 NFC Championship
Green Bay 30, Carolina 13

Green Bay hosted the Carolina Panthers in the '96 conference title game, GB's first championship game since the Ice Bowl. Brett Favre, Dorsey Levens, and Antonio Freeman starred as GB cruised.

Super Bowl XXXI
Green Bay 35, New England 21

Green Bay returned to the top after a 29-year absence! Brett Favre threw touchdown passes to Andre Rison, and Freeman, and Desmond Howard returned a kickoff 99 yards for a touchdown to spoil New England's comeback bid after a Pats' TD pulled the score within 27-21. Reggie White's three sacks of Pats' QB Drew Bledsoe sealed the deal.

Prominent players and their top #100 ranking include:

#3 – Brett Favre
#7 – Reggie White
#40 – Antonio Freeman

#49 – Dorsey Levens
#50 – Chris Jacke
#54 – Edgar Bennett
#88 – Mark Chmura
#90 – Frank Winters
#95 – Gilbert Brown

2010
10-6

2010 NFC Championship
Green Bay 21, Chicago 14

As the #6 wild card entry, Green Bay had to beat the Eagles and Falcons just to get to the NFC championship. A pair of interceptions by Sam Shields, and an unlikely pick-six by B.J. Raji were the key plays in the 2010 NFC championship. Raji, "the Freezer" evened the score after William "Refrigerator" Perry embarrassed the Packers in the '80s.

Super Bowl XLV
Green Bay 31, Pittsburgh 25

In Super Bowl XLV – Nick Collins had a pick-six, Greg Jennings caught two TD passes from Aaron Rodgers, while Jordy Nelson snared another. Clay Matthews' stripped the ball from Rashard Mendenhall, and Desmond Bishop recovered in a key defensive play.

Prominent players and their top #100 ranking include:

#4 – Aaron Rodgers
#18 – Charles Woodson
#30 – Jordy Nelson
#34 – Clay Matthews
#36 – Mason Crosby
#43 – Nick Collins
#46 – Greg Jennings
#61 – James Jones

Sources: Wikipedia, www.packershistory.net

WHAT MIGHT HAVE BEEN?

Some players are fortunate and get to enjoy long, productive careers. Brett Favre, Ray Nitschke, and Bart Starr, are among Packers who readily come to mind. But other careers are cut short, and in some cases long before the player's Packers career ever even really got started. This chapter is devoted to 10 of the former Packers that fans were left to think, "What might have been?"

Creative Commons

NICK COLLINS, S

(Packers seasons 2005-11)
Collins was a second-round pick out of tiny Bethune-Cookman in Ted Thompson's first draft as Packers GM. His play steadily increased until he became a two-time Pro Bowl selection. His pick-six off Steelers QB Ben Roethslisberger, helped Green Bay to an early lead in Super Bowl XLV. But the following season, Collins suffered a severe neck injury tackling Carolina RB Johnathon Stewart, and it was the last time Collins would ever suit up for the Packers.

Creative Commons

Creative Commons, Joe Bielwa

Creative Commons, Neon Tommy

MARK D'ONOFRIO, LB

(Packers season 1992)

D'Onfrio, a standout linebacker and team captain at Penn State, was a second-round selection by Packers GM Ron Wolf. A severe injury forced D'Onfrio to retire. Fortunately, he's lasted much longer in the coaching ranks, where he is currently an assistant linebackers coach at the University of Houston.

JERMICHAEL FINLEY, TE

(Packers seasons 2008-13)

Finley, a third-round selection out of Texas, was a defensive player's nightmare: Too fast for linebackers to cover, and too strong for defensive backs to tackle. He burst on the scene in 2009 with a 6-catch, 159-yard performance in the Packers' playoff loss to Arizona. He suffered a season-ending knee injury against Washington in 2010, missing out on the Packers' Super Bowl championship run. A healthy Finley caught 55 passes in 2011 and 61 in 2012 before suffering a career-ending spinal cord injury in 2013. The Packers haven't had a TE like him since.

JOHNATHAN FRANKLIN, RB

(Packers season 2013)

The Packers needed to revive their sagging ground game, and so even after grabbing Eddie Lacy in round 2, Thompson drafted UCLA RB Franklin one round later. Seeing as how Franklin was a First-Team All-American and Second-Team All-PAC 10, it's not hard to believe how TT found this talented back too hard to resist. Franklin topped 100 yards rushing in a Week 3 loss against Cincinnati, and suffered a severe neck injury later that season against Minnesota. He retired in the off season.

Creative Commons

Creative Commons

Mark Forsch Collection

EDDIE LEE IVERY, RB

(Packers seasons 1979-86)

Georgia Tech's star rusher was phenomenal, rushing for 356 yards (an NCAA record at the time) against Air Force in 1978. But after a standout college career, as a Packer, Ivery ripped up his knee not once, but twice against the Chicago Bears, becoming an ultimate "what might have been" in Packers' lore. That he is still the Packers' 13th-all-time leading rusher is a testament to how great Ivery might have been had it not been for his knee injuries.

TIM LEWIS, CB

(Packers seasons 1983-86)

Lewis, a first-round selection out of the University of Pittsburgh, quickly became a solid starter on some pretty mediocre Packers' defensive squads. He led or shared the team lead in interceptions in 1983 and '85, and brought back a pick-six 99 yards against the Rams in 1984 (a Packers record). But a severe neck injury – notice a tragic theme here? – suffered in a Monday Night game against the Bears in '86 proved to be a career ender.

TERRENCE MURPHY, WR

(Packers season 2005)

Ted Thompson had a knack for drafting terrific wide receivers, and Murphy, a second-round pick out of Texas A&M, may well have proven to be as good as later Packers receivers, and early round draft picks, such as Greg Jennings and James Jones. But alas, we'll never know. Murphy was injured on a kickoff return by the Panthers' Thomas Davis in a helmet-to-helmet hit (legal at the time). You guessed it – it was another neck injury.

STERLING SHARPE, WR

(Packers seasons 1988-94)

I was hesitant to include Sharpe on this list, since he did enjoy a seven-year playing career, and is ranked #25 out of the Packers' 100 All-Time-Greats in this book. Even still, that he ranks #2 all-time in team receptions, and third in yardage, one can't help but wonder where he might have ended up had he played longer. Many believe he would have even approached the legendary Jerry Rice's totals – Sharpe was that good.

DEREK SHERROD, OT

(Packers seasons 2011, 13, 2014)

Taken one year after Iowa standout tackle Bryan Bulaga, Sherrod, a first-round selection out of Mississippi State, and Bulaga, were supposed to be the Packers' bookend tackles for a decade – much like Chad Clifton and Mark Tauscher before them. But it didn't end up that way. He broke his leg against the Chiefs, missed the entire 2012 season, and never really recovered from the gruesome mishap.

AARON TAYLOR, G

(Packers seasons 1994-97)

Taylor, a first-round selection out of Notre Dame, enjoyed a six-year career (four with the Packers, two with the Chargers), which was pretty amazing for a player plagued by knee injuries. But still, one was left to wonder how good he might have been.

ACKNOWLEDGMENTS

First and foremost, I wish to thank Shawn Williams for his terrific layout and design work on this Packers project. He is a very talented graphic designer, and his skills, and input, played a key role in making this publication a reality. And he's a great neighbor to boot. Thanks Shawn!

Second, I wish to thank editor and former Waupaca County Post reporter Jane Myhra. As a published author of several novels, Jane had some very useful advice in terms of marketing the book.

I also need to acknowledge one of my online groups – the Writer's Network – for their assistance in terms of organizing the book, determining the number of pages, and so on.

I also want to thank Rich Palzewic, editor of Packerland Pride, and Multimedia Channels (MMC) for their permission in allowing me to re-use material that began as a four-part series in PP, and has since been embellished upon (sometimes considerably) for this book.

In the statistical and related information cited in this book, the author relied on his memory as much as possible, using sources such as Wikipedia links largely to check years a given player played for the Packers, and to confirm certain statistical information.

MANY thanks to Packers fans who supplied images for this book: the previously mentioned Rich P., plus Mark Forseth of Iola, WI; Tony Prudom, Appleton; Mike Worachek, Card and Coin/Packer City Antiques, Green Bay; and Chris Nerat, Heritage Auctions. Plus a Don Hutson photo is courtesy of the Green Bay Packers.

I also need to recognize that three Lombardi greats passed away during the writing of this book: tackle Bob Skoronski, running back Jim Taylor, and tackle/guard Forrest Gregg.

No list of acknowledgments would be complete without mentioning my wife, Debra. Knowing I am a big Packers fan, she did not have any problem with my pursuing this project even though the financial payoff was completely unknown.

Finally, I thank God for the writing talents he's given me that I am only too happy to share with others.

Happy reading.

DEDICATION

This book is dedicated to the memory of my father, Francis Jacquart. I shared a lot of Packers stories with my dad over the years, and one of the most memorable occurred in April 2007. Brett Favre was still the Packers' quarterback, and he was clamoring for Packers GM Ted Thompson to go after Randy Moss, as the star receiver was reportedly being shopped by the Oakland Raiders.

Some would have hailed landing a talent like Moss, but the gifted WR was probably almost as famous for his showy antics and outspokenness as he was for his acrobatic catches in traffic. It was that part of his character, not his ability that ruffled the feathers of a soft spoken father like mine. He watched great Packers' squads of the '60s that continually put team ahead of their incredible individual talent, so my dad didn't have any use or respect for a brash player like Randy Moss – no matter how good he was.

My dad was terminally ill, and speaking was not something he did a lot of anymore. But when I mentioned that the Packers were "considering" signing Randy Moss, my dad didn't have to utter a single word. The quizzical look on his face said it all... "You have GOT to be kidding?!" he was clearly thinking. I completely knew what he meant with just that single look. "Way to go, dad," I thought.

My father taught me that the TEAM always comes first. Showiness. Brashness. Cockiness. Call it what you want, but my dad didn't see any place for it on a football field. Lombardi would not have tolerated it, and my father didn't either. It was one of the many lessons he taught me about sports over the years.

Growing up in the late 1960s and 1970s, unfortunately I was more familiar with the mostly crummy Packers teams of the '70s, than the Lombardi era, which I barely recalled personally. But my dad was a very knowledgeable fan who knew those players well... everyone from Hornung and Starr, to Davis, Nitschke, Gregg, and others. He described them so well that I felt like I had seen all of them play!

Perhaps even more important, he also told me about outstanding Packers whose achievements were often overlooked in the dismal years that preceded Lombardi's arrival in 1959. (The same year I was born, by the way.) One such player was standout defensive back Bobby Dillon, who my dad relished talking about as a player who excelled on the field despite having only one working eye. It was his recollection of Dillon's great play that led me to include Dillon as high as I did in this book, which lists the 100 greatest Packers of all time. (For the record, Dillon came in 27th.)

My dad died on April 7, 2007, just days after I shocked him with that nasty Randy Moss rumor. TEAM first. Individuality SECOND. I got it, Dad. Lesson learned.

MIKE JACQUART

Francis and Mike Jacquart

ABOUT THE AUTHOR

MIKE JACQUART

Mike Jacquart is a freelance writer and editor. Prior to that, as the sole editor at Impact Publications, Inc. he wrote and edited roughly 400 continuing education trainings for the child care, adult care, and foster care fields. He was also an award-winning education reporter at several daily and weekly newspapers in Wisconsin. Mike has been published in "Packerland Pride" and "Out & About Wisconsin" magazines. This is his first book. Mike interned on The Lynn Dickey Show on Channel 11 while attending UW-Oshkosh.

elevatingeapawareness.wordpress.com
writeitrightllc.com
linkedin.com/in/mikejacquart

ABOUT THE GRAPHIC DESIGNER

SHAWN WILLIAMS

Shawn Williams is a graphic designer who is constantly developing print and digital strategies including design, photography, video to communicate all kinds of messages. He has been an art director at ad agencies creating monitor graphics, corporate branding, app development, and web design. And before that the graphic designer for *Comics Buyer's Guide* magazine and other periodicals, books, and electronic media. Shawn also wrote, illustrated a graphic novel called *Five Pounds & Screaming*. He is the illustrator of the comic strips *Simple Pleasures* and *Supe & Indy* as well as other writing and publishing projects. Shawn is a proud father of a wonderful young lady and keeper of composting worms in central Wisconsin.

shawnbrookwilliams.com
instagram.com/shawnbwilliams
cargocollective.com/shawnwilliams

Made in the USA
Columbia, SC
23 June 2019